Leading
Leaders
in **Retail**:

The Essential Guide

REVITALISING RETAIL

Leading Leaders

in Retail:

The Essential Guide

by Alison Crabb

alison crabb

inspiring the humanity of business

Published by Alison Crabb Consulting
PO Box 202
Moonee Ponds VIC 3039

Edited by Scharlaine Cairns, Charlie C. Editorial Pty Ltd
Cover and internal design: DiZign Pty Ltd
Illustrations: DiZign Pty Ltd
Typeset in 11pt Avenir Next and Noto Serif
Printed in Australia

ISBN: 978-0-6489090-2-6 (Paperback)
ISBN: 978-0-6489090-3-3 (e-Book)

A catalogue record for this book is available from the National Library of Australia

Disclaimers:
Some of the names and identifying details in this book have been changed to protect the privacy of individuals.

The URLs appearing in this book were current at the time of publication. The author and publisher are unable to guarantee the ongoing currency of any URLs included in this book.

To the many retail leaders on the
career development path

Foreword

I employed Alison Crabb in 1990 as a trainee Flight Centre rookie. It did not take long for us to realise we had a gun salesperson with the strategic thinking to match.

After just 18 months, Alison was appointed to a Flight Centre store manager role. We delegated to our store managers total responsibility and accountability for their stores' performances and profitability. This meant that they had to learn resilience and persistence, and to develop a 'can-do' attitude with an optimistic streak.

These became fundamental life lessons for Alison as she rose through the ranks, from Flight Centre store leader through area leader, state leader and national leader to have a remarkable tenure of 25 years at Flight Centre Travel Group (FCTG) – Australia's fourth largest retailer with 18,000 staff in fourteen countries globally.

The Flight Centre business model teaches all the vital retail business lessons about maximising profits and growing productivity, but also focuses on superior management of people.

Alison's leadership acumen truly shone during her tenure as the Victoria and Tasmania (Vic/Tas) leader, the largest division globally within FCTG. For eight consecutive years, Alison guided Vic/Tas to unprecedented heights, making it the most profitable division within the company. Under her leadership, the division's profits grew from $18 million to $49 million, and the number of stores expanded from 149 to 212. These achievements underscore her ability to drive growth and foster a culture of success.

In 2010, Alison received Flight Centre's prestigious Global Directors' Award in recognition of her exceptional results. This accolade reflected her outstanding leadership qualities and unwavering commitment to excellence.

So, why is there a need for this book in the retail sector today? The retail environment is more competitive and dynamic than ever before. Success hinges on having the right products; cultivating a strong, motivated team; and creating a cohesive, aligned organisation with an excellent culture. Alison's philosophy is grounded in the belief that people are the cornerstone of retail success. If you can create a wonderful culture and 'can-do' attitude, maximisation of profit and staff retention will be the resulting outcomes. Her insights into how to value, align, and reward team members are invaluable lessons for anyone seeking to thrive in this industry.

This book delves into the core principles that have driven Alison's success:

- **The value of your people in retail:** Discover how to build and nurture a skilled team, passionately committed to the organisation's vision.
- **Ensure everyone is aligned:** Learn strategies for ensuring that all team members work towards common goals, fostering a unified approach to the achievement of success.
- **Reward and recognition:** Understand the importance of recognising and rewarding your team's efforts and learn how to implement effective reward systems that drive motivation and performance.

Alison's experiences and insights provide a roadmap for navigating the complexities of the retail world. Her ability to inspire, lead, and achieve remarkable results makes her uniquely qualified to guide retail leaders through the strategies and practices that can elevate their businesses.

I endorse this book to you for maximising your business outcomes with the lessons it contains front and centre!

Geoff Harris AM
Co-founder of Flight Centre

Contents

Contents

Contents

Preface

I have known from early in my working life (if not before) that resilience is a valuable trait to have or to develop in leadership. It is not just a means of coping – it is the foundation for moving forward with a positive outlook from even the greatest challenges. My own life experience has shown me just how valuable resilience can be.

There will be times in life when you will be confronted with things to overcome and endure. Life does go on beyond those moments of challenge and the ability to 'bounce back' and reestablish confidence in yourself and those around you is what resilience is all about. It is a highly desirable trait in those who hold leadership roles and it is even more desirable if those leaders can encourage and develop resilience among the people they lead.

On the next few pages, I will share the reasons my own experience has led me to value resilience and why it has played such a major part in my life.

From the beginning

From the age of eight, I had known I wanted to be a teacher. I would set up my bedroom as a classroom, gather all the children from my street, teach them maths and English and read books as they sat on my bedroom floor. I would even deliver very in-depth school reports to their parents.

After graduating from high school, I was accepted into teachers' college and it seemed that my lifelong dream was about to become a reality.

Three years later, I graduated from teachers' college. But, instead of feeling fulfilled with the achievement of that long-held goal, I found the first few years after graduating very unsettling. I wasn't quite sure where I belonged, what I should be doing or what future direction I should take. I ended up in regional Victoria chasing a relationship which, eventually, turned out to not be as good for me as I had hoped.

Licking my psychological wounds, I returned to Melbourne hoping to settle into my teaching career.

I was still getting over the break-up of my relationship when two great Irish friends from teachers' college convinced me to accompany them as they booked a trip back to Ireland and through Europe.

When we walked into the travel agent together, both girls suddenly said, 'Why don't you come with us!' I admit that I was caught up in the moment and, somehow, with all the excitement, I left the travel agent with my deposit paid and my itinerary in my hand.

I don't quite know what I was thinking because I had enough money for the airfare but not a cent of spending money – and we were leaving in three months! But, even so, I headed home very excitedly to share the great news with my mum.

After having spent the whole of the previous week in my bedroom crying after my big break up, the next morning I left the house in search of a job and came home that night with two – working as a full-time receptionist at a car yard by day and at a local cafe on weekends.

That same night, friends introduced me to a guy named Brad who asked if I'd like to meet him for lunch the following day.

We had a nice lunch and discovered we had a lot in common. The following day, he called again and asked if I would like to go with him to a function the following night.

Over the following three months, it would be fair to say that Brad and I spent every spare moment together.

On 28 February 1989, my friends and I flew to London as planned. After a couple of weeks of staying with my aunt we began travelling through Europe, but there wasn't a moment went by without me thinking of Brad.

When I returned to my aunt's home in London after six weeks of travelling through Europe, I was surprised to find waiting for me two big bags overflowing with letters, postcards and presents that Brad had been sending to me almost daily.

Daily phone calls from Brad followed while I was staying with my aunt so, realising that I just wanted to be with him, I made the decision to come home.

I arrived home on his birthday at the beginning of May.

Brad and I set up a home together. I did some emergency teaching and worked in his retail clothing business – which, together, we built to be a very successful business.

It wasn't long before Brad popped the question and, of course, I said 'Yes' – and we began planning our wedding.

* * *

One particularly hectic hot summer's evening, I had planned to head to Melbourne so I could pick up my wedding dress the following morning, but I decided I was just too tired and too hot and would make the trip in the morning.

Brad had headed off fishing with our neighbour George and I had settled in for a quiet night watching television.

Later that night, George's wife came running down my driveway screaming that George had been in a car accident.

I hurriedly grabbed my bag and we headed straight to the hospital. On the way, I consoled George's wife, telling her that everything would be okay – but I still thought, 'Where's Brad?'

When we arrived at the hospital, George's wife was rushed to his bedside, but no one seemed to know where Brad was. It was clear only one patient had been brought into the hospital. I decided that he was probably at the police station making a statement.

I rang Brad's mum and dad to tell them the little that I knew.

Very soon after Brad's parents arrived at the hospital, two policemen walked in. They took us into a small room and gave us the devastating news. Brad had been killed instantly in the accident.

In that instant, my world was changed forever. I had lost the man with whom I thought I would be spending the rest of my life. All of our plans had suddenly ceased to exist. I was in complete shock. A call was made from the hospital to tell my mum.

I headed to Brad's mum and dad's place and it wasn't long before my mum arrived. The house was soon in chaos, with relatives arriving to console us – everyone was in shock.

This happened just three months before the planned date for the wedding and, instead, I was faced with planning a funeral.

The next few weeks were simply unbearable; so many decisions to make: 'Where am I going to live?' . . . 'What do I do now?' . . . 'Do I continue teaching? If not, what else could I do?'

The truth is, I felt like doing nothing. Even getting out of bed seemed too hard. I made every excuse possible to try to justify why I couldn't make any decisions. I could have just sat and done nothing – but I just knew I had to do *something*.

Starting again

Within a couple of weeks, I had moved back to live with my mum, which meant I was also close to my friends and family, who had mounted a 24/7 support vigil around me.

I knew I needed to start making some decisions, in particular getting back to work. I loved teaching, but I thought I needed to do something else for a little while – something that I would enjoy and that would keep me distracted from everything I was dealing with.

A dear friend suggested we plan a short holiday for later that year, maybe to Bali. She said I should get some travel brochures because that would keep my mind occupied and give me something to try to look forward to.

The following day, I went to the local Flight Centre to collect the brochures. Having always had a passion for travel, chatting with the consultant about our travel plans, I began to think, 'This wouldn't be a bad job.'

I asked the consultant what was needed to get a job in the travel industry. The requirements were a tertiary degree, to have travelled to at least three continents and to have sales experience. I was able to tick all three of those boxes.

The consultant gave me the phone number of Geoff Harris, the co-founder of Flight Centre, and suggested I give him a call.

I called Geoff that afternoon and, after a phone interview, he asked me to meet with him face-to-face the following Thursday.

Although it was a long time ago, I still remember that interview very clearly. Geoff sat at a rickety old desk in a room out the back of a Flight Centre store. I remember thinking that some of the questions he asked me during my interview were quite odd – such as, 'Can you sell?' Fortunately, selling was one of the many things Brad was brilliant at. He was a born salesman and had taught me to sell – and to sell well!

Geoff asked me a lot about my parents, where they were from, and what they did for a living. It was clear that he was trying to ascertain more about my background, my upbringing and my values: Did I have the right work ethic? . . . Was I a good culture fit for Flight Centre? . . . Did I have the attitude and determination to be successful?

When Geoff asked me why I wasn't pursuing a career in teaching, I told him what had happened three weeks before and said I just needed a chance. I promised, if given the opportunity, I wouldn't let him down.

In the back of my mind, I was thinking, 'Could I do this? Am I ready? Is it too soon? Is this even what I want to do? How do I know? What if I do let him down?'

Fast forward to the current day and Geoff remains like a father figure to me. I think it was his generosity and compassion that got me the job, rather than any skill, aptitude or ability I might have had. I also think he just felt sorry for me and wanted to give me a chance. But, before he could give me that chance, I needed to be willing to make the decision to let him give me a go. I'd had to rise above all my doubts and follow my gut – that was all I had!

I got the job and started the following Monday at the Flight Centre store in Bourke Street, in the heart of Melbourne.

Although I can't recall ever having been familiar with the term 'resilience' I think, at some level, it was resilience that helped me navigate the aftermath of my personal tragedy. By acknowledging my feelings, seeking support, engaging with and embracing change, I gradually rebuilt my life.

The new job

So that's how I became a travel consultant!

Day one of the new job involved a brief office orientation and the rest of the day was spent learning how to use the reservation system.

On day two, I dealt with my first customer enquiry. It happened to be from a young man who wanted to travel to Bogotá. Now, I don't know what was more puzzling to me – was it that I had absolutely no idea where Bogotá was, or was it the fact that the young man actually booked a trip there after speaking with me?

It wasn't long before I realised that this job was very different from anything I had ever done. It also wasn't long at all before I started to feel right at home with my new team, who were incredibly welcoming, understanding and supportive.

I could see there was something very different and special about this Flight Centre business. It had a supportive culture I just couldn't quite define.

Even though my friends had continued to rally around me, I still had low moments when I was alone – and Sunday nights were the worst for me. I would be chomping at the bit to get back to work on Monday morning so I wouldn't need to think about my grief and loss. Over the months that followed, I started to make Flight Centre friends who really became my new family. I felt cared for – and I felt like I belonged!

Empowerment and ownership were core philosophies of the Flight Centre business. I felt I had ownership of my results and my destiny. I loved the sense of passion that everyone shared, and I just felt very proud and special to work for Flight Centre.

Losing Brad was one of the most significant events of my life; many aspects of my life following his loss were shaped by it. Some of the beliefs it caused me to form have not necessarily served me well and I have needed to actively work at changing them.

My experience at Flight Centre after Brad's loss also taught me a lot about the importance of human-centred leadership – understanding that your people are humans first and employees second. Many aspects of my leadership values have been shaped by my own experience – among them, the importance of belonging, taking ownership of your choices, working hard and remaining resilient.

'Life is difficult' is the famous first line of M. Scott Peck's book *The road less traveled: A new psychology of love, traditional values and spiritual growth* (Simon and Schuster, New York, 1978). I must agree! But I want to also stress that 'Leadership is difficult' in the same way.

We can't control the experiences that life throws at us; we can only control how we respond to them, and that will always be what matters most!

Alison Crabb

Acknowledgements

The writing of this book has taken me on an incredible journey – one I could not have completed without the support and encouragement of many individuals.

First and foremost, I would like to thank my family. To my husband Shane, and my children Aaron and Matthew, thank you for your support and encouragement which enabled me to focus on this project at such a busy time in our lives.

To my business manager Lisa McKay, you have been an enormous support behind the scenes. With your incredible attention to detail and can-do attitude, you help me keep on top of everything.

Thanks to Scharlaine Cairns, my editor, for your meticulous attention to detail and guidance throughout the writing process. Your expertise has been instrumental in bringing this book to life. Thanks also to Diana Murray who has designed and illustrated my first two books.

I am forever grateful for the twenty-five years I had the privilege to spend with the Flight Centre Travel Group, and am especially grateful to the company's founders Geoff Harris OA, Graham 'Scroo' Turner, and Bill James. Joining such an amazing retailer in the early days meant I had the opportunity to watch how the business flourished. All three leaders had a profound impact on me, personally and professionally. Many of the business philosophies fundamental to Flight Centre's success are intertwined throughout this book.

Gathering feedback from a broad range of retailers was essential in the early stages of writing this book. To my retail industry clients, thank you for your encouragement and for sharing your experiences with me.

Thanks especially to CEO Daniel Agostinelli, Armando Pedruco, Adam Rudzki, and Kiane O'Farrell from Accent Group, who have all been enormous supporters of my work; Sally Craig from Kennards Hire; Robyn Casey, Jaimee Charlton, and Geoff Abbott from Spendless Shoes; Mandy David from Pancake Parlour; Jo Newman from Taking Shape, and Gerri Fleming from Peter Alexander. Your feedback has been vital in making this guide comprehensive and practical.

I am deeply grateful to the many retail leaders with whom I have had the privilege of working. Your stories, challenges, and triumphs have greatly enriched this book.

Lastly, to the readers of this book, thank you for your interest and for striving to become better retail leaders. I hope that this guide will provide you with valuable insights and tools to excel in your leadership journey.

With gratitude
Alison Crabb

Introduction

After five years as a Flight Centre store manager, I was excited to take on the first area leader role in 1995. Flight Centre Victoria/Tasmania had grown to twenty-six stores, and co-founder Geoff Harris was still leading every aspect of the business.

The area leader role represented a fantastic opportunity because I was working alongside Geoff himself, meaning I had the chance to learn from the best. He looked after strategy to ensure the business continued to grow and I looked after the day-to-day operations. I was exposed to many of the broader aspects of the business, such as identifying sites for new stores, negotiating leases and creating marketing opportunities. At that time, I even recruited novice consultants because we weren't big enough to have that function provided independently by someone else. The recruitment aspect provided one of my most valuable learning experiences, holding me in good stead in future roles. It helped me to appreciate the importance of recruitment based on attitude ahead of skill. Due to my teaching background, I also did a lot of sales and leadership training.

I consider myself fortunate to have learned so many crucial aspects of the business in my relatively early years with Flight Centre.

I spent almost four years as an area leader before taking parental leave and having my two sons. Eighteen months later, I returned to work part-time – facilitating leadership training for store managers.

The business had grown significantly by then and there were five area leaders leading various geographic areas. It wasn't long before one of those area leader positions became available – but it wasn't just *any* area leader position. The area was comprised of eighteen stores, of which only one store was profitable, making it Flight Centre's globally most underperforming area. The person who took on the role as that area leader would be expected to work at turning results around. I accepted the challenge.

Three years later, with me as area leader, the area had grown to comprise twenty-three stores and was Flight Centre's second most profitable area globally. (Refer to my first book, *The essential guide for area leaders in retail*, in which I share many of the strategies that contributed to the turnaround.)

In January 2006, due to my previous success as an area leader, I was asked to take on the role of Flight Centre Travel Group's leader of Victoria/Tasmania. It was a difficult decision for me to leave the area I was leading, because I wanted to reap the rewards of all the hard work that had turned the area around. But there were only four leadership roles across Australia similar to the role I was being offered, meaning opportunities like that didn't come along every day. If I hadn't accepted the role then, there was no saying when a role like that would be available again. So, looking forward to a new challenge, I accepted the offer.

When I took on that new role, I transitioned from being one of seven area leaders on a team to leading the team. My relationship with each of the area leaders needed to change, from being their peer to being their leader. I knew that building trust with each of the area leaders would be crucial.

By then, Victoria/Tasmania had grown to 142 stores in seven geographic regions, and was led by a team of seven area leaders and a state-based support team of thirty-three people. Just six months into the financial year, results showed that the sales and profits of six of the seven regions were down by more than $2,000,000 compared to the previous year. This was already a disastrous result.

Careful examination of the situation made it clear that the issues directly contributing to the poor results appeared similar to those I had dealt with as an area leader: inexperienced leadership; low morale; low brand standards; and a high turnover of people. Financial goals were in place, but there were no clear strategies for achieving them.

The nature of the travel business meant that, to improve results, there needed to be a heavy reliance on people. Better results couldn't be delivered without people being motivated and engaged – so that is where I needed to start.

I met one-on-one with each of the area leaders and state-based support leaders who, beneath all their frustration, I found to have an incredible desire and desperation to succeed. From discussions with them, I learned that standards and expectations were low and, due to a lack of direction, the members of the area leader and state-based support leader teams felt lost and highly stressed. Several area leaders had lost their confidence and questioned whether the role was a good fit for them. All were working longer and longer hours, constantly reacting to problems in stores and trying to fix them.

The turnover of area leaders had been almost 50% in the previous few years, with many leaving within the first eighteen months of commencing in the role. Those who had been successful store managers had struggled to find a way to make the transition to area leader.

It was evident that improvements in the people side of the business would significantly improve the other areas needing attention. Although a lot needed fixing, I started by implementing strategies to improve the work environment and stem the flow of people leaving or wanting to leave. I share some of those strategies and approaches later in this book. For example:

- continued regular one-on-ones (see pages 182–4)
- SWOT analyses (determining strengths, weaknesses, opportunities and threats; see pages 88–92)
- two-day retreats aimed at setting visions, goals and plans, and creating trust and connection (see pages 78–81)
- open communication and transparency of results (see pages 24, 82–3, 171–5 and 179–94)
- full-day store managers' planning sessions (see pages 82 and 182).

From all of my discussions I identified three main challenges that we needed to address:

1 retaining and developing people in stores

2 improving the customer experience

3 increasing the rate of conversion from enquiries to sales.

With that list of goals in mind, store managers created achievable short-term goals for their stores and simple actions to achieve them. This resulted in many great strategies being developed, but also resulted in each store manager feeling informed, inspired and supported – and having ownership, responsibility and accountability for their own plans and actions.

I started to see things improving as area leaders worked with store managers during store visits and store manager meetings to support them and help them implement their plans.

Over the following few months, results showed that the strategies were working. The improvements continued and, in eight years under my leadership, Victoria/Tasmania became the most profitable of Flight Centre Travel Group's divisions globally, growing sales from $100 million to $1.3 billion, the number of stores from 142 to 212, and profits from $18 million to $49 million year-on-year.

Outstanding results were achieved during those eight years, but leading a big business in a volatile industry was often challenging. There was the need to navigate through the Global Financial Crisis of 2007/08 (and its aftermath) and to deal with many events that had an enormous impact on the travel industry, such as multiple terrorist attacks in key destinations; and globally impactful weather conditions and natural disasters, such as ash clouds and tsunamis.

I learned that one person alone can never completely control business outcomes. There is a need for a leader to positively influence the team. I also learned that most of what impacts a business is based on the business environment that has been created, how well goals and directions have been set and communicated, and the empowerment of the business's people to achieve the set goals.

I strongly believe it is time to rethink what retail leaders are doing and what empowered leadership in retail could look like.

Over recent years, using what I have learned from my lived leadership experience, I have trained, coached and mentored more than 700 leaders in various roles in retail, from area leaders to CEOs, across retail businesses of all shapes and sizes. Regardless of the business's structure, many of those leaders were working incredibly hard but were working in isolation and for many more hours than necessary – risking burnout. Many of them were doing things the way things had always been done, without recognising viable alternatives. Goals were usually in place but there was also a lack of alignment with those goals and unclear communication of them to people empowered to develop plans to achieve them.

I am especially passionate about the area leader role, and I am certain it will always be hard for retail businesses to succeed unless area leaders are set up for success.

My first book, *The essential guide for area leaders in retail*, is filled with strategies aimed at specifically assisting area leaders in their transition from store managers to area leaders and at developing a systemised approach to their roles so they can have more impact and improve results.

My work with senior retail leaders, confirmed to me the need for this, my second book, challenging the thinking behind many outdated ways of working at a senior leadership level. I also saw this book as my way of encouraging leadership support for area leaders in their implementation of the new strategies and ways of working that I teach in my leadership programs and have included in my first book. Chapter 9 of this book is dedicated to helping area leaders improve their results, but the book also contains many practical strategies for more senior leaders to help them help area leaders to perform at their best.

Although this book contains a more strategic approach to retail operations than my first book, it still significantly focuses on people.

For twenty-five years, I successfully built great teams – of six to eight people early in my career; of 80–100 people midway through my career; and of more than 1400 people during the last eight years of my retail career.

This book contains the lived lessons and strategies gained from my experience as a retail leader, including:

- how to create a work culture to which it is worth belonging
- being a leader people want to follow
- how to trust and empower the people you lead to achieve results.

On the following pages, I will share with you the proven strategies and leadership philosophies for leading and empowering leaders that drove my results and my approach to leadership.

Some of the strategies covered in this book might already be in place in your business, but I hope I can elevate your thinking and suggest new strategies to further improve outcomes and results – and that you can take some of my philosophies and strategies and make them work for you.

Alison Crabb

How to use this book

This book is written for senior retail leaders. Depending on the size and structure of the business, your title may be state manager, head of retail, retail operations manager, national manager, general manager, or CEO. Your role and responsibilities and organisational structure may also vary.

Regardless of your title, or your specific responsibilities, no doubt you will be working closely with your leaders and teams to develop and implement your brand strategy and operational systems.

This book has been conceived as a 'how-to' guide to help challenge your thinking and show how leaders can adapt to the ever-evolving retail landscape.

All of the suggestions made in this book have been proven to work for me and the senior leaders whom I have led throughout my career. They have also helped many retailers who have taken advantage of my training and coaching programs since 2016.

Each chapter of this book focuses on a key aspect of the senior retail leadership role, and I invite you to make your own notes in the places provided throughout the book.

At the end of every chapter there is a page on which it is intended you write your 'Light bulbs'; by this I mean any points that suddenly made something clear to you (your 'ah-ha moments') and to which you can particularly relate, or that you would like to discuss or reflect upon further.

There is also a page provided at the end of each chapter on which you can note 'Actions', meaning points I have made to which you not only can relate but which you would also like to implement in your role or discuss further with your leadership team.

I encourage you to make use of those two pages in each chapter, so that you can start to create your own toolkit of ideas and actions.

Throughout the book there are also checklists and templates which focus on various aspects of leadership. These can assist you by providing a focus for reflection on aspects of your own leadership and that of others.

Part 1:

Understanding leadership and performance

Chapter 1

Defining a leader and leadership

There are many definitions of 'a leader' and of what sound and successful leadership entails. The leadership styles and behaviours that become our own are likely to have been influenced by leaders whose approaches to leadership we have experienced personally.

In my early years of leadership, I was fortunate to have some incredible role models and mentors (as well as experiencing some 'leaders' who were far from incredible and provided me with a different kind of learning experience). Whether good or otherwise, each of those leaders helped me to form my own beliefs and philosophies about leadership. I came to realise that results are always a significant reflection on the leaders and their ability to lead.

I have observed situations in which a business had consistently achieved outstanding results, but results declined when the successful leader moved on and a new leader took over. In contrast, I have also observed a struggling business that started to flourish with a change in leadership.

The influence of a leader cannot be underestimated. A great leader can create strategic direction and inspire their whole team to follow them.

As part of my research, I asked many people attending my workshops about the leaders they admired or whose positive leadership approach they had experienced first-hand. What they shared about those leaders included:

- they could build trusting relationships
- they could make people feel valued and appreciated
- they always led by example and set a standard by their own behaviour
- they were consistent, approachable and easy to communicate with
- they allowed people to make mistakes so they could learn and grow

- they had a clear understanding of the needs of the business
- they could engage their teams, and ensure team members felt ownership of the goals set and the plans implemented
- they could work in the here and now, as well as plan for the future.

In this chapter, I want to share what I have observed about leaders in retail and what I have experienced when leading people.

Whether you are leading a state-based team or a national team, many of the challenges remain the same. I have worked with and interviewed many senior retail leaders and have found that all have experienced similar challenges, with the source of many of those challenges being the leading of people. As any product becomes more readily accessible and more competitors enter the market through various channels, it will be your people who make the difference.

The role of every business leader should be to create a great environment in which everyone wants to be – and to remain. It is paramount to maintain relationships with store teams (and that works towards fulfilling their 'human need' for 'significance'; which will be discussed later [see pages 54–5]).

Whenever I talk to other business leaders, I ask them what is happening in their business, and what some of their greatest challenges are. In one way or another, the answers usually relate to people: attracting good people; retaining good people; inspiring people; or finding ways to make people more productive. There are probably other common challenges but, in one-way or another, it seems to always come down to 'people, people, people'.

I can relate to all these challenges and, over the years, have needed to deal with all of them. However, my approach has always been to work from the inside out. What I mean by this is that the management of teams of people can be made a lot easier by understanding those people more deeply, appreciating that they are humans first and employees second, understanding what matters most to them and working towards providing an environment that supports those things.

To lead a business, you need to become an expert at leading people.

Your 'history book'

Lived lessons in leadership

I met Rhona Miller while participating in a leadership program she facilitated during my very early days as a leader. Even though this was thirty years ago, that program and Rhona's teachings had a profound effect on me.

It was Rhona who taught me about the concept of the 'history book'.

She taught me that our 'history books' contain all the significant and, sometimes, seemingly not-so-significant events that have happened in our lives. I learned that those life events shape our beliefs and behaviours and, ultimately, our results – not just in business, but in all aspects of our lives. I found this to be a powerful concept and it has had a significant impact on my leadership.

Whether, as individuals, we have had different life experiences from others or similar life experiences to them, we will have all formed different perceptions and beliefs about those experiences. No one else sees the world precisely as we each see it.

The more we can each understand our own personal 'history book' and acknowledge that each of us has a completely different one, the more we can understand why we all perceive the same situations differently.

In this book's 'Preface', I shared a significant piece of my own history book, upon which many of my own life beliefs and behaviours were formed. That is the part of my history book where I learned to be resilient and which, admittedly, also gave rise to some personal fears and limitations.

Rhona, thirty years my senior, became one of the most influential people in my life. Many of my approaches to leadership are based on what she has taught me and she is responsible for shaping many of the leadership philosophies I hold to this day.

Rhona turned eighty-nine in 2024 and has remained my very close confidant and dear friend.

Your 'history book' refers to all your experiences throughout your life. Important aspects of your history book may include how you were raised, the environment in which you grew up, and the relationships you had with your family members. All of these experiences shape your beliefs and behaviours. Sometimes, you continue patterns from your upbringing and, sometimes, you rebel against them.

One of the most important aspects of the leadership role, underpinning everything else, is building trust with and within your team to ensure strong relationships. Part of building trust is understanding each of your team members' history books and allowing your team to understand yours. For example, if you had hard-working parents, this may have shaped your own work ethic and contribute to your approach to leadership.

As part of a team we can all share the same experience but, because of our different history books, we can each perceive the same situation quite differently. These differences are often at the heart of conflict in teams. A great way to build trust is if leaders and team members can get to know and appreciate the differences between the members of the team (their differing history books), can manage their sometimes conflicting perceptions, and can ensure that all team members gain an appreciation and understanding of how they all differ from each other.

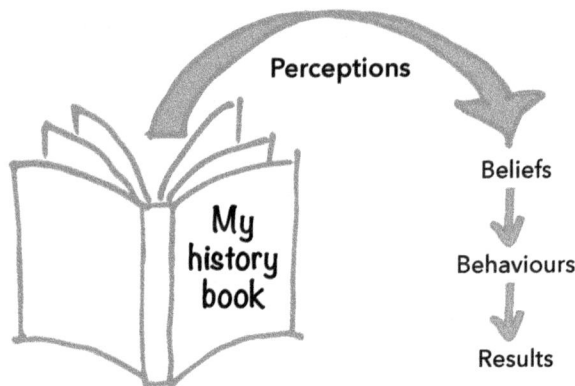

Perceptions

My history book

Beliefs

↓

Behaviours

↓

Results

There are many ways that team members can get to know each other's history books.

I do introduce the concept of 'your history book' in many of the leadership programs I facilitate. Depending on the size of the group, I may ask each person to bring along an item that has personal meaning and significance and that they are happy to share with the group. This allows everyone the opportunity to gain an understanding of what each individual values most in life. For example, someone might bring along a precious piece of jewellery that was a gift from a grandparent who played a significant part in their life; or it may be a photo of their children, indicating how important family is to them.

I have been amazed by some of the items that people have shared. I recall someone bringing along a handmade backgammon board, which was more than seventy years old and had been passed down from generation to generation. It represented the way Sundays had been spent by fathers and sons, playing backgammon through the generations.

The connection between team members this activity can spark is incredible, leading them to understand each other better and connect on a different level.

When we can each share our personal history book (a little of it, or a lot), we begin to build meaningful and trusting relationships. I can't imagine building a connected team without the sharing of history books being an integral part of the foundation that will help the team perform at its best.

From this sharing exercise, team members can often learn that they are more alike than they are different.

American author and speaker Dr Brené Brown has brought discussion of the concept of vulnerability into the sphere of business leadership. Her research has led her to write many books, including *Daring greatly: How the courage to be vulnerable transforms the way we live, love, parent, and lead*.[1] Her TED talk 'The power of vulnerability'[2] has been viewed more than twenty million times.

In the past, vulnerability was widely considered a weakness. Ultimately, if your team members feel that they need to mask their feelings, or 'suck it up' and soldier on, they will constantly clad their psychological 'armour' for fear of being seen as weak. However, allowing your team members to be vulnerable doesn't mean just allowing them to always 'let it all hang out'. Vulnerability requires boundaries and trust if it is to be an asset.

In her book, *Daring greatly*, Brené Brown wrote:

> *Vulnerability is about sharing our feelings and our experiences with people who have earned the right to hear them. Being vulnerable and open is mutual and an integral part of the trust-building process.*[3]

1 Brown, Dr B., *Daring greatly: How the courage to be vulnerable transforms the way we live, love, parent, and lead*, Avery Publishing Group, New York, NY, 2012.

2 Brown, Dr B., June 2010, 'The power of vulnerability', TED, viewed 3 August 2024, <https://www.ted.com/talks/brene_brown_the_power_of_vulnerability>.

3 Brown, Dr B., 2012, op cit. p. 45.

The more vulnerable you can be with your team, the more you grant permission for your team members to also be vulnerable. I have worked with many senior leadership teams who have gained enormous benefit from getting to know not only their own team but also the other senior members of their business at a human level. That has been the catalyst for building healthy, trusting relationships and helping improve team alignment to achieve goals. Understanding this leadership concept can make an enormous difference.

Self-reflection: Leading leaders checklist

The descriptions in the checklist below have been designed to help you reflect on areas in which you may be able to grow and improve as a leader. Put a tick in the column provided beside each description that you see provides an opportunity for you to focus and improve.

LEADERSHIP SELF-REFLECTION CHECKLIST	
I am clear on what defines me as a leader.	
I have a good understanding of my strengths as a leader.	
I have a good understanding of areas of my leadership that I can work on.	
I have a trusting relationship with each member of my team.	
I know the history and background of each member of my team.	
My team members feel comfortable sharing challenges from outside of work.	
I invest time in building relationships outside of my direct team.	
I encourage my team members to spend time getting to know each other.	
I feel comfortable offering honest feedback to individuals in my team.	
My team members feel comfortable offering me honest feedback.	
I believe receiving honest feedback will help me grow as a leader.	
My team members feel comfortable offering feedback to each other.	
I feel comfortable offering my leader honest feedback.	
I spend time helping each of my team members improve their leadership.	
Besides my leader, I have mentors whom I can ask for advice.	

Leaders are role models

If you reflect on your retail career, it is likely you will have taken the usual career path, shown below.

The career path to retail leadership

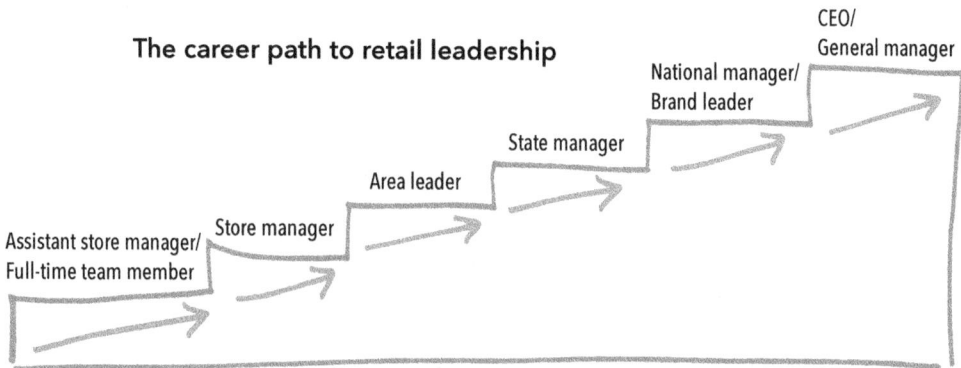

Your path might differ from the exact path described by the diagram, but it is likely to have been some recognisable version of it.

As you grew in your roles (as shown in the diagram), you are likely to have had leaders you looked up to and hoped you could be like one day.

Thinking about your past leaders and their influence on you will help you decide what type of leader you become and the type of leader you model to others.

- Who were the leaders you looked up to and now model your leadership on?
- Who have been (and continue to be) the mentors you look to for guidance?
- Did you have a leader who, by their actions, showed you what *not* to do?

The further up the leadership ladder you go, the more people will look to you to lead by example and show them the way. It is important to acknowledge that, as a leader, you too are a role model. Your people will look up to you, just as you looked up to your own leaders.

The more senior your position within the business, the more knowledge and experience you have gained or will gain. However, while leadership can be powerful, the adage 'Knowledge is power' can only be of real benefit once relationships and trust have been established. If we fail to build relationships, it can become much more difficult to implement strategy (especially if that requires making changes).

When working with business leaders, I highlight the importance of leading by example. Although this could be considered 'basic leadership 101', it is very easy to forget that people are always watching you, even when you think they aren't. This is especially true the more senior the role you hold.

I ask the leaders I work with which of their own leaders they admired and which have positively impacted their own leadership approaches. Often, the answer is not someone with a high leadership profile and media presence but their current senior leader or someone they have worked for in the past. I often encourage them to share with the leader they identified the positive impact their influence had on them. (Giving thanks and praise is also a great leadership quality.)

How great leaders lead

From working with them, I have observed the attributes and behaviours of several successful retail leaders and have found them to have much in common. I have also asked many of the people they lead what qualities and attributes they admire most in their leaders. Their answers included:

- they are able to build strong relationships at all levels, regardless of the role
- they have a thorough understanding of operational challenges and experience in the brand's frontline
- they 'walk their talk'
- they have the ability to recognise great results
- they communicate clearly and provide honest feedback
- they have the ability to receive honest feedback
- they engage and inspire their team
- being consistent in their leadership and remaining calm under pressure

- they psychologically invest themselves in the role, taking full ownership of the brand, its success, and the part they play in it
- they encourage those they lead to also have a sense of 'ownership'.

These leadership qualities don't amount to rocket science, but they highlight that people admire their leaders most for how they make them feel, as well as what they do.

COMMON SENSE OVER CONVENTIONAL WISDOM

Common sense and conventional wisdom are related concepts, but they are different. Working with many retailers over recent years, I have consistently seen a reliance on conventional wisdom over common-sense solutions. But 'common sense over conventional wisdom' is one of Flight Centre's tenets.

Conventional wisdom refers to the generally accepted beliefs and opinions held by a group. It is often based on tradition or authority, rather than on direct personal experience or observation. Conventional wisdom can be helpful as a starting point for understanding a particular subject. But, it can also be misleading or inaccurate and based on outdated information or biases. If it is no longer the best way to approach something, relying on conventional wisdom alone could result in wasted time and financial resources.

Common sense refers to practical knowledge and sound judgment based on personal experience and observation. It is often intuitive and can be applied to a variety of situations. Common sense is based on an individual's ability to reason and make logical connections between different pieces of information. It is often used to make quick decisions or solve practical problems. Common sense can often prove more reliable than conventional wisdom, especially when decisions about complex, unfamiliar or unprecedented situations need to be made.

Because it is grounded in personal experience, an appeal to common sense can help leaders think critically and creatively about the problems confronting them, rather than simply relying on outdated or incorrect beliefs.

Lived lessons in leadership

One of the most challenging roles of my career was leading the region known as 'Vicmania' (Victoria/Tasmania) during the global financial crisis (GFC) in 2007–2009 and its aftermath in the 2009–2010 financial year.

During the two years preceding the GFC, we had achieved outstanding sales and profit growth in the Victoria/Tasmania region. The number of stores had grown from 142 to 160 and we were looking forward to another successful year.

Early in the 2008–2009 financial year, I had started to see the effects that negative media reports were having on consumers. Business confidence was on the decline and, within a couple of months, revenue was declining daily. The signs were obvious that it was going to be a challenging year – one that would require a change in strategy.

In this situation, it was important for senior leaders to create more certainty and provide direction, so that every area leader and store manager could create a plan for their stores to deal with the effects that the decline in enquiries and travel conversations was having on sales. Store managers were the ones feeling the effects first-hand.

I gathered the region's support team and area leaders and, together, we came up with a plan in which, rather than stripping costs out of the business, we looked at the places where we were wasting money.

This was followed by a store manager focus day, for which we gathered all the store managers together. The store managers were given the same direction as the support team and area leaders and were asked: 'How can we reduce costs in stores without impacting our people or our customers?' and 'How can we convert more enquiries to sales in the domestic travel market?' I need to say that I was thrilled with some of their ideas and how they were able to implement them.

In times of crisis there are always opportunities. It is a case of 'when given lemons, make lemonade'. That is where common sense over conventional wisdom has served me well. When the rest of the retail and travel industry was 'zigging', we 'zagged'.

- During that year we recruited more people, so adequate time could be spent training them in preparation for the time when the demand for international travel returned to normal.

- Shopping centres were feeling the pressure as more and more stores became vacant. This made it the perfect time to sign new store leases, extend existing leases and provide landlords with more certainty – which enabled us to negotiate better rents.

alleviate potential problems and make implementation of ideas as seamless as possible.

This is especially true if a leader is moving to a new business or a new role within the same business. Each time someone leads a new team, or changes roles, even within the same business, they must go back to begin at leadership Level 1 – and the requirements of each level must be progressed through and fulfilled before they can move to the next level.

If you behave as if you are a 'Production' level leader (Level 3) before you have transitioned through the 'Permission' level (Level 2) and established solid relationships of trust with the team you are leading, making changes to strategy becomes much more difficult. Sometimes making changes quickly is necessary – but implementation can only happen quickly and seamlessly if time is taken to build relationships first.

When people trust you, they will follow you.

Identifying how you can improve your leadership ability

The checklist on the next two pages is a summary of all that has been discussed in this chapter. It may give you insights into what you are doing well and highlight the growth opportunities you could consider for improving the quality of your leadership. Read through the listed expectations and responsibilities and circle the appropriate response each time. Some of these may not be specifically aligned with the responsibilities of your role, but still may provide food for thought regarding opportunities for growth.

- If you always fulfil a described leadership expectation, circle 'Y' for 'Yes'.
- If you fulfil a described leadership expectation only some of the time, circle 'S' for 'Sometimes'.
- If you never fulfil a described leadership expectation, circle 'N' for 'No'.

Completing the checklist, will enable you to easily see which expectations or responsibilities you marked 'Yes', and which you marked 'No' or only 'Sometimes'.

Some of the expectations and responsibilities that you marked 'No' may not appear to be important to you right now but, as you continue to read through this book, I hope you will recognise them to be areas on which you can focus to improve your leadership.

LEADERSHIP CHECKLIST			
EXPECTATION OR RESPONSIBILITY	RATING MYSELF		
Marketing and brand			
I have a thorough understanding of who our customers are.	Y	S	N
I have a thorough understanding of our customers' needs.	Y	S	N
I have a sound understanding of our product, marketing, and merchandising.	Y	S	N
I ensure the product is appropriate for our brand and our customers.	Y	S	N
I have experience in the frontline of our brand.	Y	S	N
I take full ownership of all elements of our brand (including positioning, product development, store growth and operations).	Y	S	N
I ensure our marketing plan is clear and effective.	Y	S	N
I ensure consistency across all marketing channels.	Y	S	N
I have a twelve-month product strategy.	Y	S	N
I take ownership of brand fit-out and ensure it meets brand standards.	Y	S	N
Strategy			
I have a sound understanding of operations.	Y	S	N
I work with board/senior executives to set high-level brand strategies.	Y	S	N
I work with board/senior executives to implement high-level brand strategies.	Y	S	N
I ensure our brand strategy is operational and is implemented.	Y	S	N
I ensure that product, marketing and sales strategies are aligned.	Y	S	N

(Continued on next page)

(Continued from previous page.)

EXPECTATION OR RESPONSIBILITY	RATING MYSELF		
Communication			
I am able to build relationships at all levels of the business.	Y	S	N
I hold regular, effective brand stakeholder meetings.	Y	S	N
I work with and am understood by all key stakeholders.	Y	S	N
I help create alignment with goals and plans at all levels of influence.	Y	S	N
I break down obstacles to our brand's success.	Y	S	N
I regularly communicate results to teams.	Y	S	N
I engender brand pride and success through communicating a clear brand vision.	Y	S	N
Growth			
I champion growth.	Y	S	N
I work with leaders to ensure brand strategy is implemented to ensure growth.	Y	S	N
I regularly review KPIs to look for opportunities for improvement.	Y	S	N
I am proactive not reactive when results are not in line with expectations.	Y	S	N
People development			
I inspire the people I lead.	Y	S	N
I am committed to people and leadership development.	Y	S	N
I have a succession plan for all leadership roles.	Y	S	N
I show appreciation and recognise great performance.	Y	S	N
I am able to provide honest feedback to help my people improve.	Y	S	N

Light bulbs

Actions

Chapter 2

The performance pyramid

As I outlined in my first book, *The essential guide for area leaders in retail*, seeing the pyramids of Giza for the first time, when I travelled to Egypt in 1993, had a profound impact on me – one I will never forget!

The Pyramids of Giza were built in 3000 BCE and it is believed that they took 85 years to complete. Thousands of years later, they are still standing. The reason for that is they were built on the strong foundations of a solid limestone rock plateau under the sand, with solid limestone and granite blocks used for the construction. It is those strong foundations and the use of the strong, stable, solid pyramid shape for construction that has enabled them to remain standing to this day, so tourists like me can visit and wonder at their magnificence.

In the years after my trip to Egypt, I came to realise that the leading of great teams in business is very similar to the building of a pyramid.

The foundation of a business needs to be built by focusing on the business environment first. It is the environment of the workplace that provides the foundation for the strategy that then needs to be formulated. Once decided, that strategy needs to be implemented. The strength of the established business environment greatly impacts how well any business strategy can be designed and implemented. Results are achieved based on the success of the environment's foundation as well as on the strategy and its implementation.

Results

Implementation

Strategy

Environment

Since 2016, I have worked with thousands of people who hold leadership roles at all levels of retail and non-retail organisations. Regardless of the background of the participants, I start all my workshops or programs by explaining this performance pyramid. The first session is always devoted to helping leaders understand the importance of environment and strategy, and the strategy's implementation with the team working together to achieve results.

It is paramount to business success for senior leadership teams to appreciate the importance of *all* levels of the performance pyramid. So, let's look at each of the layers of the 'pyramid' in more detail as they relate to business.

Environment

In business, great teams must be built on stable, strong foundations. These foundations are part of what I call the business 'environment'.

The 'environment' of any team or business is often intangible – something that you can feel, but you can't touch or quantify. It might be hard to describe or explain but, if you pay attention when asking someone what they love about their job, their answers usually relate to the environment and will most likely include a description of how they feel about the organisation and the leader for whom they work. Your stores need to be more meaningful than just being a location within four walls.

Much of this book contains strategies for building your environment. Ultimately it is your people who drive results, so the workplace environment needs to be one of which your people want to be a part. People need to feel valued and appreciated and to have a high level of trust in their leader.

In his book *The advantage: Why organizational health trumps everything else in business*,[5] Patrick Lencioni uses the term 'health' of the organisation to refer to what I call the 'environment'.

---

5   Lencioni, P., *The advantage: Why organizational health trumps everything else in business*, Jossey-Bass; Wiley, San Francisco, CA, 2012.

Lencioni says of organisational health that:

> *It's not at all touchy-feely, and it's far bigger and more important than mere culture. More than a side dish or a flavor enhancer for the real meat and potatoes of business, it is the very plate on which the meat and potatoes sit.*[6]

Concentrating solely on revenue and profit will never enable a business leader to attract the best people or help retain them. Revenue/profit is one measure of business success. But the way people feel about the organisation and about their leaders has enormous impact on the morale of the team – and it is the morale of the team that impacts on how well the people do their jobs and look after their customers. It is that which ultimately delivers results – and it is that which needs to be the focus.

Even though I am convinced that the building of a great business must start with the business environment, I often witness this aspect of a business being the most neglected. If you want to attract great people to your organisation, it is necessary to have an environment in which people want to work. How people feel about the business's environment will determine how engaged they are when working in it and whether they will choose to stay or to leave.

Understanding that people are human beings first and employees second, and understanding what matters most to them, leads us to understand those people more clearly and enables us to set about creating an environment in which their needs are met. That will then be an environment in which they feel valued and are inspired to deliver their best work.

Case Study: **Matthew**

Matthew worked as a casual team member for a large retailer while completing his studies. He enjoyed his work and the members of the team with whom he worked.

After about six months, and after a change of store manager, he was beginning to disengage and wasn't showing the same level of enthusiasm he had shown previously.

---

6   Ibid., p. 3.

Because of the work I was doing with area leaders in the same organisation, I was curious as to what could have been causing his change of attitude. I asked him how he was doing, and whether he was still enjoying his work.

He said that, since the change of store manager, the store just didn't feel the same for him.

I suggested he speak to someone in his team and asked him if there was someone in the store with whom he enjoyed working and from whom he felt he could seek advice. Considering he had an assistant store manager, a store manager and an area leader, I was surprised to hear that the person with whom he felt most connected was his state manager, Charmaine. It made me even more curious when I realised that this was someone in the business that I imagine he may only have seen very occasionally.

I asked him why she was the person he had suggested, and his response was, 'She treats me like a real person.' I asked him to elaborate, and Matthew's own words were:

> Well, the first time I met her in the store, she asked me what I liked to do outside of work, and I told her that I was a state cricketer, and I would love to pursue a career in cricket.
>
> A couple of months later she was in the store when I was working, and she came and spoke to me. She remembered my name and asked me how my cricket was going. I couldn't believe she remembered me! She is the only person at work who has ever asked about me and treated me like a real person. It's always about the store budget and making money.
>
> Whenever Charmaine is in the store, I always want to try harder for her.

I found this to be a fascinating insight.

The higher the level of the role you attain in an organisation, the more relationships with those around you will continue to matter. In fact, they matter more and more! Those relationships are crucial if you want to know what is *really* going on at every level of the business – from the store level to leadership.

Having a connected leadership team, sharing high-quality relationships, working together and building connection and trust will significantly shape the environment and assist in implementing the business strategy.

The more senior you become in an organisation the more you will need to also focus on the next level of the pyramid – the strategy. You will be involved in the setting of the strategy for the business. But, regardless of your level of seniority, you are still leading people and paying attention to the environment will still remain crucial. Before you begin to work on your strategy, remember that creating an environment of which people want to be part remains the responsibility of every leader – and ensuring your business's 'environment' is sound provides a strong foundation on which to build.

The strategy

As well as a great environment, a successful retailer needs a great strategy – a simple, easy to implement plan of action designed to assist with achieving set goals.

Retailers invest heavily in marketing, products, and technology to attract and retain customers. All of these are vital for the sustainability and growth of the business, but a business strategy is needed to optimise that investment.

A business strategy is like a roadmap. We need to know where we are and where we are aiming to go – and the strategy is the map outlining the way to get there. Having a clear, workable strategy creates focus and direction, and bestows ownership and accountability on everyone tasked with implementing it.

Although the business will have an overarching strategy, each leader within the business should be able to take the organisation's business strategy and apply it to their own business plans. They can operationalise the organisation's strategy in their own approaches to the business and have some level of accountability for the strategy's implementation. This is really about everyone being aligned with the same goals. (Refer to Chapter 5 where alignment with goals and strategies is discussed in more detail.)

- Many retailers were reducing their advertising and marketing budgets, making it an ideal time for us to negotiate better advertising rates.

- I increased the marketing budget to take advantage of the incredible travel deals that airlines were forced to offer in an attempt to entice people to travel.

- Time and money was invested in training our leaders so they would be ready when demand bounced back.

These strategies all served the business well. Below are the figures reflecting the profit results from that time.

'VicMania' full-year profit results
2007–2008 (the financial year leading into the global financial crisis): **$33,000,000**
2008–2009 (the financial year of the global financial crisis): **$27,000,000**
2009–2010 (the financial year after the global financial crisis): **$42,000,000**

Why do many retailers keep doing what has always been done?

When I see retail leaders instructing their teams with what I perceive to be outdated practices, I ask those leaders why they do what they do. They usually reply, 'We have always done it that way.' This is an example of relying on conventional methods instead of considering more contemporary, often more efficient and effective alternatives.

How do we challenge our thinking if we are not getting the desired results? I have observed instances in which it would be beneficial to question and review the conventional approach/attitude, but it remains unchallenged. The following are some examples.

1 AREA LEADERS *MUST* MAKE MORNING CALLS TO STORES EACH DAY

Insisting area leaders start every day by calling all their stores seems to be a time waster. In the case observed, these calls were designed to remind store managers to hit their daily budgets and were a mandatory direction to the area leaders from their leader.

My research across state managers, area leaders and store managers has shown that:

- area leaders and store managers do not enjoy making or receiving daily calls

- there is no evidence that these calls positively impact results. If they did, stores would be hitting their budgets every day.

- many store managers feel demotivated, micromanaged and disempowered by receiving a call *every* morning

- the making of daily calls has become just a box-ticking exercise for conducting fluffy conversations, which are of no consequence.

If an area leader calls each of his/her stores daily, assuming there are nine stores to call (and many area leaders could have more), and they spend 10 minutes on each call, that is an hour and a half every day – which adds to a full day each week.

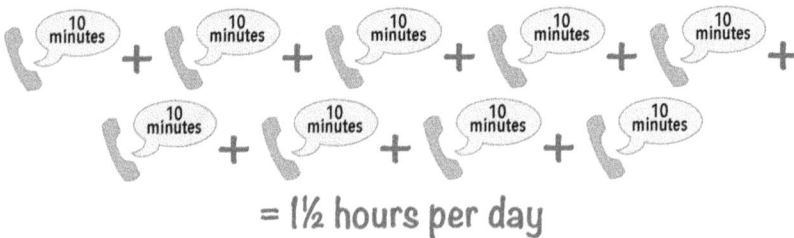

= 1½ hours per day

There is no evidence that this investment of time has any impact on the stores' results and common sense suggests that this time could be better spent elsewhere. That is not to say there is no place for calling stores at the beginning of the day, but there needs to be a more strategic approach to these calls. A common sense approach would be for store managers to call their area leader if they don't have what they need or don't know where to focus to hit their daily budget. That would be a better use of time and be more empowering for the store managers.

If a store is significantly behind its budget expectations for more than a couple of days, it may also be appropriate for the area leader to visit the store and have a business conversation with the store manager.

2 AREA STORE MANAGER MEETINGS ARE *TOO* EXPENSIVE TO RUN REGULARLY

I often hear resistance to holding regular face-to-face store manager meetings. The reasons given for that resistance are that 'they are costly', 'they take managers away from stores', and 'they require the store managers' shifts to be covered'. However, I believe rethinking that mindset will provide a great opportunity to positively impact results. I believe face-to-face store manager meetings are one of the best (and cheapest) ways to impact results and positively improve retention of store managers. I share more about store manager meetings in Chapter 12, 'A system for communicating' (see pages 186–93).

3 IT IS MORE COST-EFFECTIVE TO HAVE A HIGH PERCENTAGE OF CASUAL PEOPLE WORKING IN STORES

While a large casual workforce provides flexibility when managing rosters and costs and, admittedly, is necessary in the retail industry, having a high percentage of casual workers presents a whole set of other problems that can prove costly.

Rethinking the mix of casual and full-time team members can provide many benefits and be more cost effective in the long run. One of the biggest impacts on retail results is having effective store managers in every store. The right store manager can deliver outstanding results. The wrong one can destroy results, damage your brand's reputation and add to the turnover of people employed in the store.

Not having a store manager in a store, especially in A-grade sites, can also be just as costly. One of the great pressures for retailers is the need to have a cohort of future store managers for managing new stores when they are opened, or filling store manager vacancies when they arise. If more than

70% of your workforce is casual, you only have a small pool of people ready to take on store manager roles, or you will be forced to put people into the roles of store managers when they are not adequately trained or prepared.

It makes sense to prioritise strategies that will enable you to have a pool of potential store managers ready to fill roles. The same principle applies to filling area manager roles. The more high-quality and experienced store managers there are, the bigger the pool to draw from when filling area leader roles.

What savings could you find in your human resources and recruitment team if you were able to have a more engaged workforce who were imagining a long-term career in retail?

It seems to be common sense to rethink the mix of your workforce, especially in your flagship or larger trading stores, so that there are more full-time people who will be more engaged, have better product knowledge and can see a career path within the business. While this may increase your wage costs, it can lead to better results and will provide for effective succession planning which, in turn, will reduce the time you spend filling store manager vacancies. Ultimately, it will result in you having better quality leaders in stores delivering better results.

4 WAGES ALIGNING TO SALES

I understand that managing costs is crucial to retail results and requires careful consideration, but the resistance to spending money on wages has always baffled me. It is a 'chicken or egg' situation – wage costs and sales revenue are interdependent, with one affecting the other, but it needs to be considered which is to be made the higher priority.

Should sales team members' rostered hours depend on increased availability of budget resulting from targets having been met, or should the rostered hours be increased with the aim being to increase sales because targets have not been met? For example, if you are a shoe retailer and a customer wants to try on a pair of shoes, the customer can't try on the shoes without speaking with a salesperson who will give them the correct size. Having more people on the floor at peak times, such as weekends (even though wage costs are higher), can dramatically and positively impact sales results. Rosters should be based around the volume of foot traffic through stores, rather than sales covering wage costs, so that the chance of converting a shopper to a purchaser is increased (remember 'the chicken or the egg').

We all appreciate that wage costs must be managed. However, I often see people wandering around a retailer's support office, making coffee, chatting with colleagues, etc. People in those support roles are not subject to the same wage cost pressure as the store teams. This is not to deny that support roles are essential, but it is the people working in stores who make money for your business. When retail results are not on track, reducing wage costs in stores is the lever that gets pulled most, yet this is the lever that has one of the biggest impacts on sales.

Are there opportunities to question conventional wisdom and apply common sense to the situations you encounter? The four examples I have just chosen to highlight will be further explored throughout this book.

The five levels of leadership

Case Study: David

I worked with David, a very driven and motivated retail brand leader who was achieving great results. Due to his great results, he was asked to take on an underperforming brand within the business. David was thrilled at the opportunity to make a difference and to make use of everything that he had learned in his previous roles.

When he started in his new role, David identified that there were quite a few areas needing attention if sustainable growth was to be achieved.

With all of David's experience, he quickly went into 'fix-it' mode, which included restructuring the team and replacing some people within it. He also made several quick changes to the brand strategy.

David felt that he 'knew' what needed to be done – so away he went.

It didn't take long before he began to struggle. Although the strategies he had put in place were well-intended and made good business sense, and he was clear regarding what was causing the poor results, he noticed that people were starting to disengage and weren't doing what he needed them to do. People issues were beginning to appear.

He was finding it difficult to get the team to 'buy in', which was causing him great frustration. He received feedback that his people didn't trust him and had even become fearful of him. They were uncertain whether their jobs were safe. Many didn't understand the 'Why' behind some of the decisions David was making.

Over the next few months, David lost some very good people. He realised that his well-intended plans to prepare for growth had backfired. He started to lose confidence in himself and questioned his own ability.

The more David from the Case Study above shared with me what had happened over the previous few months, the clearer the cause of his issues became to me.

Often, significant change is necessary when turning around an underperforming business. Despite his good intentions and apparent understanding of the brand's problems, David had been so focused on processes, strategies and solutions that he had neglected to establish trust with his people. Regardless of your leadership experience or the results you have achieved as a leader, your people will only follow you if they trust you.

David soon realised that he had failed to get to know his team, build relationships, and ensure that the team trusted him. He hadn't asked questions of the team members around him, and had not brought his team on the journey with him, so results continued to suffer.

In my one-on-one coaching and my workshops with senior leaders and executives, who usually have many years of experience, I often use the model provided by John C. Maxwell in his book *The 5 levels of leadership: Proven steps to maximize your potential*.[4] I like Maxwell's model because it clearly articulates what happens when no investment is made in relationships before strategies are implemented.

Maxwell's five levels are, perhaps, best explained by me using the following diagram:

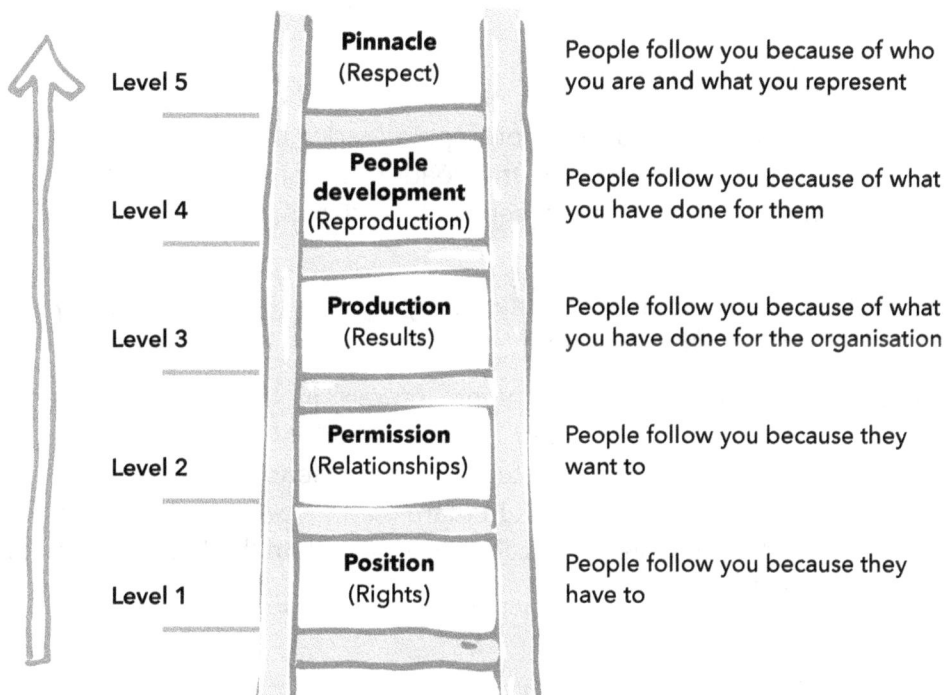

Level 5	**Pinnacle** (Respect)	People follow you because of who you are and what you represent
Level 4	**People development** (Reproduction)	People follow you because of what you have done for them
Level 3	**Production** (Results)	People follow you because of what you have done for the organisation
Level 2	**Permission** (Relationships)	People follow you because they want to
Level 1	**Position** (Rights)	People follow you because they have to

LEVEL 1: 'POSITION'

Whenever someone is appointed to a leadership role, that person starts at Level 1 as Maxwell has described it. Even if a person has years of experience as a leader, each time someone starts a new leadership role or leads a new team, they start back at Level 1. In other words, they have been given the title of 'leader' and appointed to the role but, in the eyes of their team members, they have not yet earned it. Real influence is still to be developed, but they already have the authority that goes with their title and position.

---

4   Maxwell, J. C., *The 5 levels of leadership: Proven steps to maximize your potential*, Hachette Book Group Limited, New York, 2011.

Level 1 is not where you want to lead from; having people compelled to consider you as their leader – for example, 'I'm your leader, so you will do what I say.' People do what these leaders say simply in order to ensure they are paid, to keep their jobs, and to avoid being reprimanded.

Although every leader starts at Level 1, their aim is to establish relationships, improve their credibility as a leader and move up through the leadership levels.

LEVEL 2: 'PERMISSION'

Level 2 is about the human relationships a leader builds with the team. When relationships are strong, the leader is considered trustworthy and team members tend to agree with and support any leadership decisions made.

Good relationships increase the team's loyalty and the feeling of mutual trust they share with their leader.

A leader at this level shows genuine interest in team members and gets to know each of them better on a personal level. Building a good relationship – one based on mutual respect – leads to a happy work environment and an improvement in team spirit. However, that does not necessarily lead to positive results. Results depend on the leader's growth towards leadership Level 3.

LEVEL 3: 'PRODUCTION'

This level is about leadership based on the achievement of measurable results. Leaders at this level make things happen and have been proven to get results. For this they have earned the respect of their team.

This level follows Level 2, which depends on the building of good interpersonal relationships and recognition of the fact that the team is vital to the achievement of positive results. Only when the team members take steps together, believe in one another, and trust each other will it be possible to implement strategies that will lead to achieving financial goals. To make their visions a reality, Level 3 leaders depend on both their good relationships with their team members and the respect earned from their record of success.

LEVEL 4: 'PEOPLE DEVELOPMENT'

At Level 4, leadership is about developing team members and engaging with them. A growing business needs Level 4 leaders.

Because these leaders understand the importance of developing the members of their team, they spend about 80% of their time, energy, focus and resources coaching and developing team members so they, too, will become leaders. That leaves only 20% of their time to be spent on their own productivity. In contrast to Level 3 leadership, this means letting go.

The main challenge for Level 4 leaders is to put the growth of others first – even before their own development. The more leaders that are trained, the more productive the teams to follow will be. Team members who benefit from the training and development will appreciate what their leader has done for each of them personally. Some of those 'mentor relationships' are likely to last a lifetime and will contribute to and consolidate a healthy business environment.

LEVEL 5: 'PINNACLE'

This level is the culmination of leading well on the other four levels. Leaders at this level have reached the top of their possible leadership status – a status based on a foundation of respect. People follow them because of who they are and what they represent. That respect has been earned and developed through their actions and decisions, along with the character they displayed in their leadership role. These leaders are the ones who remain in people's thoughts even after they leave the business – they live on in the organisation with a kind of 'legend' status.

The Case Study about David (pages 17–18) illustrates what can happen if a leader works at a level of leadership beyond what their team members accept they have attained. John C. Maxwell would have described David as attempting to be a Level 3 leader while operating as a Level 1 leader. As a result, the implementation of David's great strategies, and what could have been achieved to improve results, was slowed down.

Working with the five levels of leadership

When working with senior leaders and executives who have lots of knowledge and experience and who are keen to make strategic changes quickly, referring to Maxwell's '5 levels of leadership' model can help

Implementation

I have added the important layer of 'implementation' to the performance pyramid that originally appeared in my first book, *The essential guide for area leaders in retail*.

The more senior you are in the business, the more you will be involved in setting the strategy. But it needs to be remembered that a great strategy is pointless if it is not implemented effectively. Every leader at every level of the business is responsible for the strategy's implementation.

The greatest inhibiter to the implementation of a strategy is usually the environment. If morale and trust are low, and if the team is not aligned, it is likely that the strategy will not be implemented to its full potential and the desired results will not be achieved.

Results

Every retailer is focused on achieving results. Whether it is sales growth or profit growth, there is always an outcome that everyone is aiming to achieve.

Results matter!

But, having observed many organisations in many different industries, I have noticed a huge emphasis on the discussion of results. Most executive meetings are consumed by discussing key performance indicators (KPIs), with this taking up the majority of the meeting time. Hours of store visits and one-on-one discussions (commonly referred to as just 'one-on-ones') are spent trawling through reports on those KPIs.

Results are an outcome and, if you think about it, you can't directly control your results with any certainty. What you can control is where you choose to focus. My experience has shown me that the most impactful areas on which to focus are:

1   improving your environment

2   improving your key business strategies

3   improving how strategies are implemented by paying attention to the environment.

The diagram below illustrates the idea that focusing on the environment and strategies indirectly leads to focusing on results.

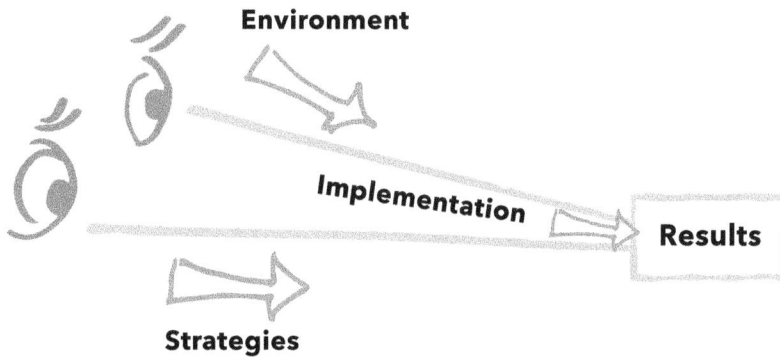

Environment, strategy, implementation and results working together

Successfully achieving results through implementing your strategy will rely heavily on the health of your environment. You could have the best-documented strategy in the world but, if there isn't alignment and a common focus among the members of your leadership team who feel collectively responsible for achieving common goals, you will spend a lot of your time trying to get everyone on board and encouraging them to work towards the same ends. That can be time-consuming and frustrating.

Your results reflect how well you have managed to provide an environment of which everyone in your organisation wants to be a part. When your team works in a positive, cohesive environment, their engagement increases, and your strategies will be easier to implement.

It is a cycle. When the environment is one of which people want to be a part, results follow and success improves how people feel about the environment. Everyone benefits when they work for a profitable and successful business.

Throughout the chapters of this book, I will share ways to create a highly productive and engaging environment and business strategies that will help you achieve results.

Light bulbs

The performance pyramid:

Actions

Part 2:
Building your
environment

Chapter 3
Building community

Why 'tribal' connection matters

I have always loved AFL football (Australian Football League) – especially my own team, the Western Bulldogs.

Many Australians are passionate about an AFL team. It wouldn't be unusual for one of the first questions asked of someone arriving from another country to be, 'Which AFL team will you support?' Attempts would then be made to convince the new arrival why they should support a particular team. Australian Football is part of the culture and fabric of Victoria. Many would argue that it is the glue that holds Victoria together.

The AFL is made up of eighteen clubs. Each club works hard to grow its membership base, from which a significant part of its revenue is raised.

There are certainly some benefits to being a season-ticket-holding member of your football team – cheaper entry to games, discounts on club merchandise and access to finals tickets if your team are participating. However, receiving these benefits is not what motivates people to become members of their clubs.

The main motivation is the sense of belonging to a community or feeling part of a tribe: building friendships with other like-minded club members; proudly wearing your club colours to games to display your support; and sitting together with like-minded people at games to cheer on your team. It's these shared human experiences that matter far more than anything else.

If retail businesses can understand how a similar sense of connection can also be of benefit to them and they are able to strategically create opportunities for their 'tribe' to connect, build a sense of belonging and feel part of something bigger, that would form the basis of a crucial strategy for improving retention and engagement – and would make work both fun and purposeful.

Lived lessons in leadership

When I worked at Flight Centre, an area of stores led by an area leader wasn't known by a geographical name, such as 'North Sydney', 'Inner Melbourne', or 'Regional Queensland'. Each area was given a 'spiritual name' symbolising what it was hoped that 'community of stores' would stand for. At that time, I was an area leader in Victoria where we had area names like 'Dynamite', 'Northern Lights' and 'Elite', to name a few. Tasmania was appropriately named 'Island force'. Globally each state or region also had a name of this kind to identify it.

Queensland was known as 'Heartland' due to the global support office being located there. Western Australia, South Australia and Northern Territory were considered to be one combined division which was known as WASANT.

Leading 'Geronimo'

The area I led was called 'Geronimo', named for a proud and prominent nineteenth-century leader of the Apache Nation of North America. Considered to have been a great leader, Geronimo led his people's defence of their land against the military might of Mexico and the United States, always exhibiting extraordinary courage and determination.

I loved that name for the area because it resonated with what I wanted the area to stand for.

Along with an area name, each area had a logo that was used by the area leader for all communication.

'Geronimo' people loved being part of that community and everyone loved the healthy competition engendered as area competed against area to win awards across the brand – state versus state, as well as area versus area.

Leading 'Vicmania'

When I became Flight Centre's national leader for Victoria and Tasmania, the area leaders and I decided that our tribal name would be 'VicMania' (a combination of Victoria and Tasmania).

We also launched a new vision with which everyone was aligned and that inspired purpose in what we did:

Courage • Pride • Growth
Inspiring lives every day

Globally

By then, each division globally also had a name, so it had become 'tribe versus tribe' on a much larger scale. The United Kingdom region was known as 'FCUK' (I will leave the reasons for that to your imagination).

The global competition between 'tribes' became real when we came together at our annual global gatherings, held at exciting destinations around the world. Typically, the top performing 10% of each division globally would be awarded a 'golden ticket' to the global gathering.

If you were a global award winner, you would be called up on stage at the official dinner to receive your award.

I was thrilled that 'VicMania', the 'tribe' I led, received the award for most profitable division eight years in a row and was awarded most improved in seven of those eight years. The only year in which we didn't improve was the year of the global financial crisis, when no division improved.

It was a huge thrill for me to be up on stage with all of my 'tribe' to receive our awards. Everyone agreed that being acknowledged for successfully representing their 'tribe' was an enormous honour and every member of the team was thrilled.

Admittedly holding a global gathering and flying people from all across the globe was a costly exercise, but it was also the biggest driver of company results because everyone worked hard to earn an invitation.

The investment made by Flight Centre to hold a global gathering was significant – flying up to 2000 people from locations around the world to meet in one chosen destination. But that undertaking worked to motivate individuals and teams to perform well enough to earn their invitation to the prestigious event, resulting in millions of dollars in profit. It was by far the company's biggest motivator and driver.

What I have described from my own experience might appear a simplistic approach (though expensive at the extreme), but the simplest aspect of the strategy – giving areas and divisions identifying names and logos – enabled team members to develop a community feeling for their region and their workmates. It was an almost tribal feeling! Everyone felt part of a team and the mindset of 'tribe against tribe' and tribal leadership resonated widely, fostering healthy competition against other 'teams', from state to state, division to division, and area to area. The most important thing was that every opportunity to create a sense of community and belonging at every level was utilised.

Areas competed against each other to be recognised for the highest achievements in regard to various KPIs, and all monthly results nationally across the brand were communicated to everyone else. It was healthy competition on a very large scale – and competition remains an important aspect of the Flight Centre culture today.

Results matter, but regardless of how senior your role in an organisation, don't underestimate the need everyone has to feel part of a community and of what is achieved. Maintaining motivation and purpose becomes much easier if an inclusive approach is taken.

What is tribal leadership?

The term 'tribal leadership' is usually used in anthropology to describe the leadership structure and practices within a group of people who share a common culture, traditions, history and identity. Defined in that way, the leadership approaches that can be described by the term vary widely, depending on the specific tribe and its traditions, but some common features include the following.

- Placing a strong emphasis on community and group identity (tribal leaders often prioritise the needs and wellbeing of the entire tribe over individual interests).
- Leading by example and setting a positive standard for the rest of the tribe to follow.
- Placing a strong emphasis on preserving their people's culture and traditions (and, often, responsibility for passing down those traditional practices to younger generations).
- A tendency to be communal and not hierarchical.

In retail, whether you are leading an area of eighteen stores or a brand with one hundred and fifty stores, the fundamental essence of applying tribal leadership remains unchanged.

The diagram on the next page is an attempt to illustrate the analogy being made and to equate the retail leadership structure with a tribal leadership structure. (Of course it is the overall structure that is being modelled here.

The function of store teams cannot be equated with the internal variety, workings, dynamics, or diversity of family relationships.)

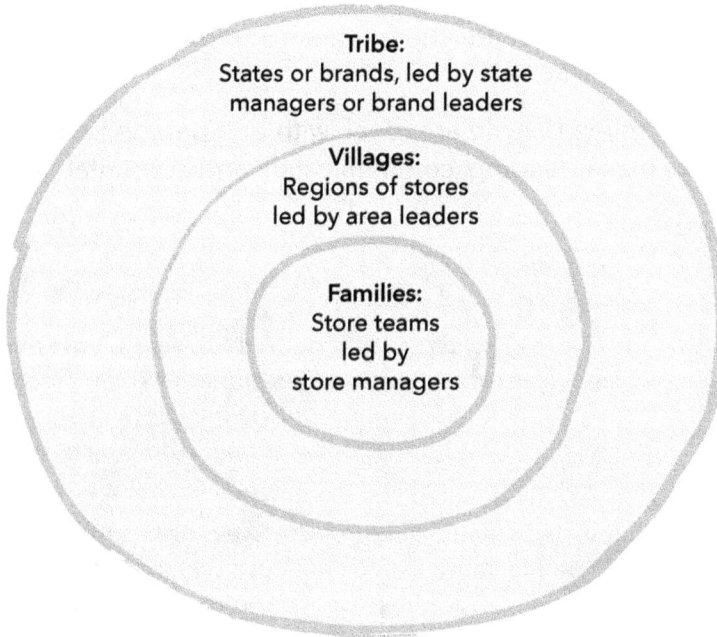

Tribe:
States or brands, led by state managers or brand leaders

Villages:
Regions of stores led by area leaders

Families:
Store teams led by store managers

Focus on small to grow big

Building sustainable growth is one of the biggest challenges for a growing retailer with big expansion plans. Without systems and structures having been put in place, growth can often turn to chaos. As more people are added to the team, accountability and responsibility can become challenging. But, if the necessary systems and structures are in place, growth can become manageable and sustainable.

So, how do you maintain teams of a manageable size, so everyone feels a sense of belonging and is part of a community?

Having the right structure, made up of small teams, is worth considering, especially for your in-house support teams. If you have large marketing or finance teams, the creation of small teams within those teams can assist greatly. The small team structure also helps with recognising accountability and responsibility. It is very easy for someone who is performing under the level expected of them to go 'under the radar' if they are part of a large team.

The creation of leadership positions within the small team also creates an extra career opportunity for those wanting to grow in their careers to develop leadership skills.

Teams of five to seven people are ideal, with one person being the team leader. That size makes leading, communication and accountability simpler.

Case Study: Amy

I coached Amy who was the leader of a large well-known global travel tour company. At that time, she was completely frustrated by her reservations team which was primarily made up of individuals from Generation Z (born approximately 1995–2012) and Generation X (born approximately 1965–1979).

Amy shared with me her annoyance at the way the members of the reservation team seemed to check in and check out each day, doing the bare minimum and not displaying much interest or effort to go above and beyond the minimum that was expected of them.

My view of Amy was that she was a great leader and genuinely wanted to be successful. As I began to understand her situation, the key contributing problem became clear to me.

I asked her about the structure of her team. She described her twenty reservation consultants, all of whom reported directly to her. As I asked her for more details about that structure, Amy herself began to understand exactly what had been contributing to her frustrations.

We discussed how having a team of twenty people meant that she couldn't create a cohesive sense of community. I used the analogy of being a parent of twenty children. You couldn't possibly know who'd had a bath, who had done their homework, etc.

Humans work best when they belong to a small team, of ideally five but no more than seven people. A team of that limited size means they develop a strong sense of belonging and feel part of that team.

I worked with Amy for the next six months and we developed a structure in which she promoted four of the team members into team leader roles, with each having four team members reporting to them. In so doing, we had created four smaller teams within Amy's team, and each team leader reported to Amy.

This didn't mean that Amy wasn't responsible for the overall results of the reservations team, but it meant she had four key people to work with and develop – and they each had the same responsibility as each other within the smaller team they each oversaw.

Each team member belonged to their own small identifiable team. They felt connected and that they were part of something. Healthy competition was fostered between teams and they would compete to exceed their own and each other's KPIs. Engagement and retention improved and sales growth was almost instant.

Relationships across leadership teams

I work extensively with senior retail leadership teams. Members of a typical leadership team hold roles across a business's various functions, such as marketing, product development, merchandising, human resources, finance, and operations.

Often, little time is spent on leadership teams getting to know each other, creating real depth and trust in their relationships, and considering the important decisions for which they are responsible and with which they need to align.

A senior leadership team can be viewed as a kind of 'tribe' or 'community', with attention still needing to be paid to its environment (see Chapter 2) so its members will be aligned and working to achieve the same goals. This applies to area leaders and also to the retail support teams.

Area leaders need to see their stores as a community, but all retailers need to understand the concept of tribal leadership (refer to page 42). Each support team should also feel like a small community.

Everyone needs to feel a sense of belonging and to feel valued and appreciated for their contribution to the business – especially in an industry where a large proportion of the workforce is young casual workers.

The need for connection

How can you find ways to allow your areas and states (tribes) to connect – not just via your communication systems but also through meaningful human connection that makes them feel part of a 'tribe' or a community?

How can your people also connect to the important work they do and appreciate the difference they can make in the lives of their customers?

Lived lessons in leadership

As part of my leadership development at Flight Centre, I was given the challenge of turning around the results of the most underperforming group of retail stores in Australia, known as 'Geronimo'. It's fair to say that the area's eighteen stores were not performing at all well – there was high consultant turnover, a lot of customer complaints and very low morale among the teams, which all contributed to declining sales. In fact, only one of the eighteen stores was showing a profit.

During my store visits, I set about determining what was causing the poor results. It was on just my second store visit, on the first day, when I had a breakthrough moment which influenced not only my perspective regarding the eighteen underperforming stores but also my perspective on my own career and my attitude towards the people with whom I dealt.

As I was waiting in the store, a customer walked in to make an enquiry. She waited patiently to be acknowledged. Eventually, a consultant lifted her head and asked the woman whether she needed help. The customer proceeded to explain that she needed to fly to Bangkok in the next few days.

The immediate response, delivered by the consultant with a very disinterested tone was, 'Well, if you are leaving in the next few days, it is going to be very expensive!'

Hmmm, I thought that was an interesting response. Not the best way to build rapport with a customer!

The consultant began to ask a few more questions, but it felt a little bit like she was taking an order at a fast food restaurant: 'Any preference for an airline?' ... How long will you be away? ... Do you need accommodation?' I was expecting to hear her say, 'Would you like fries with that?'!

The consultant then asked, 'How many people are travelling?'

The lady replied, 'Well, it will be two adults travelling to Bangkok and two adults and an infant returning.'

'Wow,' I thought. 'How amazing!' It sounded like a very special travel enquiry – bringing home a baby!' Surely the consultant was going to get excited!

But no, her level of interest and her demeanor didn't change at all. She just proceeded to tap away at her computer, preparing a quote as if she was typing a shopping list.

I could feel my temperature rising and, at that point, I couldn't resist interrupting. I stood up, walked over to the customer and said, 'I'm so sorry to interrupt, but I couldn't help overhearing your enquiry. It sounds like you are bringing home a baby.'

The woman's face lit up and she proceeded to share her story. She and her husband were adopting a little girl. They had been waiting three years for this moment and it was finally about to happen. She described to me how difficult the process had been and how she had begun to think this moment would never arrive. From what she told me, it sounded like they had been through a very long, drawn out and emotional process. I couldn't help but become a little emotional myself and could only imagine how difficult it had been for her and her family.

I wished her well; she took her written quote and left the store.

When the woman described in the text above left the store with her quote, I had a lightbulb moment about the important work travel consultants do and the important role they play in the lives of their customers. That moment changed my perspective regarding what was important to me and how I needed to lead my people. It altered the course of my business life!

That interaction sowed the seeds for the vision to which I adhered as the area leader of 'Geronimo'. That vision was best articulated by the following words, thought to have originated in the African or the North American First Nations culture:

It takes a village to raise a child.

From the moment I gained that perspective, I aimed to ensure every consultant had a sense of purpose and was connected to the important work they did and the community of which they were a part.

That vision centred on empathy and caring for both the people I led and our customers, as well as providing a sense of belonging and connection. That tenet is one I still hold close and share at every opportunity.

IT TAKES A VILLAGE TO RAISE A CHILD

This ancient proverb teaches us eternal truth.

No man, or family is an island. We'd all like to think we live in a place where people care about others- where people pitch in to help when things get rough.

It's pretty awful when you feel like you are all alone and whole world is against you. Life is a lot easier when; you are part of a network of friends and family, a community, a village.

It does take a village, to raise a child and weather the storms of life. If we want that kind of support, the place to begin is with ourselves. Community, like charity, begins at home.

If you don't know someone in your area, you can take the initiative. You can go and chat to a new person and welcome them; you can ring someone that has had a tough month and offer some support. You can reach out to your own team and start building community. You can make a difference to someone else.

There are many things that we just don't have much control over. But building a great area is something that we can do, right now, in the place where you are now.

You start building a good neighborhood when you yourself decide that you will be a good neighbor.

Light bulbs

Actions

Chapter 4

People: The greatest business asset

Have you ever wondered why some retailers dealing in similar markets or industries seemingly thrive, and others don't?

Such external factors as business being 'tough' due to the economic climate, increased costs, the falling value of the dollar, or the continual growth of online retail competition are usually blamed for failure and poor results. Although some of these external factors have real effects, I think they can also be used as excuses or as a smokescreen to prevent examination of the real reasons some businesses perform better than others.

Massive demand fluctuations during the COVID pandemic forced retailers to rethink their strategies. Many problems were exposed that had existed before the pandemic but then needed addressing. Following the COVID-pandemic, retailers may have still been feeling the hangover of dwindling margins, increased costs, supply chain challenges and, most notably, finding great people to fill leadership roles.

High turnover of people has reinforced the genuine need retail businesses have to engage and develop their leaders if they are to retain them.

As I emphasised earlier, throughout my time in business, one key factor has consistently trumped anything else in determining a business's success or failure. That factor is people. I have always professed that the people of any business (especially its leaders) are at the heart of its results, particularly when external factors impact the business. Over the last few years, retailers have seen first-hand the positive impact of having teams of great people as well as the cost of not having enough of them.

Having worked in an industry that relies on its people to deliver its results, I know that the one key factor for driving both good and bad results is people.

The results of a business suffer if the business:
- doesn't have the right people in the right roles
- struggles to retain the best people
- struggles to attract people to fill roles
- doesn't invest in career development
- struggles to maintain people's motivation to deliver results.

Appreciation of the value of your people is the foundation of everything else in leadership. If you were building your dream house, you would want it built on solid foundations because, if it wasn't, cracks would appear and, worse, it would not be as solid as it needed to be and could fall down. Businesses are no different. When you build a business on solid foundations, you build something that can withstand whatever external or internal issues threaten to undermine it.

Your people are everything in business. It is in your people that your solid business foundations are built. Without great people it is difficult for a business to thrive.

The right people in the right roles

Businesses can achieve outstanding results when the right people are in the right roles, working in a positive environment and leading in an inspiring and empowering way.

Attracting and keeping the right people are the biggest challenges for all levels of retail business. Post-COVID, this was exacerbated. Many people found that being in lockdown for extended periods caused them to reevaluate their choices – especially their career choices and their decisions regarding how they live and work. The choices made are often at the heart of the business challenges regarding attracting and hiring the right people.

Tips for recruiting the 'right people'

A clear recruitment strategy can help you avoid making poor choices when hiring or promoting people for specific roles – but you can never have a foolproof recruitment strategy. Following are some tips that may help you to recruit the right people.

1 Having the right people at all levels of leadership is vital. You first need to ensure that your recruitment team is made up of the right people to be making the recruitment decisions for your business.

2 Senior retail leaders often started work in stores, probably as casuals, and worked their way up the ranks. So, having the right people in stores, imagining their career path within the business, will ultimately increase the size and potential of the long-term selection pool for filling senior leadership positions.

3 Recruiting the right people for area leader roles is crucial. Area leaders are influential in retaining store managers and their team members, and will play a large role in those people staying in stores longer.

4 For all senior roles, ensure you have a clear succession plan that you review frequently. Have regular career conversations with potential leaders and provide early opportunities for them to develop their leadership skills.

5 Recruiting from within the business to fill senior roles should always be the preference. Great people will stay longer if they see opportunities for personal growth within the business.

6 Even if all the required skills for a position aren't evident in a candidate, motivation and attitude are crucial. Skills can be developed, but attitude often can't be.

7 A great recruitment plan requires attention from the operational leaders. Your recruitment team is a valuable resource but, ultimately, decisions about filling leadership roles must be left to the operational leaders.

8 If you are constantly needing to recruit externally to fill leadership roles, that is a sign that your succession planning strategy needs attention.

Retaining and motivating the 'right people'

What I have learned from each success I have witnessed or of which I have been a part is that, regardless of the size of the team, the foundations for building success remain the same. It all depends on people.

Understanding why people come to work

The six core human needs

In the middle of last century, American psychologist Abraham Maslow expressed a theory of five 'needs',[7] the pursuit of which dictate human behaviour:

1. physiological needs (air to breathe, food, water, sleep, etc.)

2. safety needs (security of self, of family, of property, of health, of employment, etc.)

3. love and belonging needs (connection with others, friendship, family interactions, sexual intimacy, etc.)

4. esteem needs (boosts to personal self-esteem, improvement of self-confidence, achievement of goals, the gaining of respect from others, etc.)

5. self-actualisation needs (self-improvement, creative self-expression, etc.) which are, in essence, all about personal growth and our contribution to the world.

Maslow ranked his five needs in order on a pyramid shape with the basic needs on the bottom levels (first the physiological needs and, next, those related to safety). The other needs continued to be ranked, above the basic ones. This was intended to show how our needs gradually change as each of them is fulfilled.

The needs at each level must be met before the remaining needs higher on the pyramid can also be met.

Based on his fascination with human motivation and behaviour, American career and business strategist Tony Robbins took some of what Maslow had professed, combined with some of his own theories and discoveries, and proposed his own 'six human needs'.[8]

My interpretation of Tony Robbins' six core human needs follows.

---

7 Maslow, A. H., *Motivation and personality*, Harper & Row, New York, NY; and London, 1954.

8 Robbins, A., "Discover the 6 human needs", *TONY ROBBINS*, 2024, viewed 3 August 2024, <https://www.tonyrobbins.com/mind-meaning/do-you-need-to-feel-significant>.

1 **The need for certainty:** Striving to experience comfort and gain a level of stability, predictability and safety in life – which helps minimise the stress of uncertainty.

2 **The need for variety:** Enjoying trying new things and striving for excitement and change – which helps relieve boredom, predictability, and stagnation.

3 **The need for significance:** Striving to gain a sense of significance and importance in other people's eyes – the objective being to create a sense of identity and to feel valued and appreciated.

4 **The need for connection:** Striving to make deep connections with people – to fulfil the need to belong, to love, and to be loved by others.

5 **The need for growth:** Striving to learn, experience, and grow mentally, emotionally, and spiritually in different ways throughout life.

6 **The need for contribution:** Giving back, contributing, and making a difference in the world.

Robbins' Six Human Needs					
Certainty	Variety	Significance	Connection	Growth	Contribution

The 'six human needs', as described by Robbins, are not 'desires' or 'wants'. They are psychological needs that we consistently work on satisfying at both conscious and unconscious levels of awareness. They influence our deepest motivations and determine how we prioritise our decisions and actions throughout our lives. In fact, every single day we are unconsciously striving to meet these 'needs' – with varying levels of success.

The more our needs are met, the greater our happiness, joy, and fulfilment. But, when the needs are not met, we feel unfulfilled and dissatisfied. However, because most of this happens at a subconscious level of awareness, we probably don't even realise why we might be feeling miserable.

It is not hard to see how all six of Robbins' human needs can be met in a workplace environment.

Lived lessons in leadership

After having spent four years as a Flight Centre area leader, I became pregnant with my first son, Aaron and, soon after, came my second son, Matthew. I stayed home to look after my young boys for a couple of years, then returned to Flight Centre and took on a part-time role as a leadership trainer. My role was to facilitate the store manager program for new store managers.

As the new store managers shared with me the challenges they were experiencing, I soon realised it was the people side of the business that the managers struggled with most. I was consistently hearing the same things from the managers in each group with which I worked. These leaders were all so focused on their results that they had lost sight of why they had become leaders in the first place. They had also lost sight of the importance of creating an environment of which their people wanted to be a part.

What the people working in the stores desired more than anything else was connection and to feel part of a community – to know that what they did mattered and that they were doing important work. The store managers' focus seemed to have shifted away from providing that.

Later in my leadership journey, I became fascinated with some of the work of Tony Robbins and his perspectives on the 'six human needs'. That growing fascination coincided with the time I returned to full-time work and to my true professional love – the role of area leader.

In 2004, I took over as leader of the underperforming area known as 'Geronimo' (see pages 57–9 for details).

As I went from store to store, all the classic signs of what caused stores to underperform were evident, including low morale, high customer complaints, high turnover of people and poor brand standards.

I could see that the store managers had lost sight of their purpose, as well as being consistently fearful of not hitting their sales targets. The work environments in these stores were not positive ones and, as a result, were not environments in which people could succeed – and they fell short of fulfilling the needs expounded by Tony Robbins.

Team members were leaving the stores in droves. The frustrations of the store managers were compounded by constantly needing to train new people.

What I had learned when facilitating team leader training, combined with understanding what seemed to matter most to these store managers, led me to recognise an opportunity to perform my area leader role very differently.

Based on the poor area results, I had nothing to lose by trying something new!

Reflecting on my time training store managers, as well as on numerous one-on-ones with store managers, I realised that people working in the travel industry didn't just come to work to sell travel. Selling travel was the vehicle for them to meet their human needs – and the meeting of those needs was why they came to work.

I also realised that work was where people sought significance, growth, connection, and a sense of belonging. Gaining these understandings represented nothing less than a profound revelation for me. I had unlocked the key that would make a difference to people in the workplace and how they felt about their work. Combined with my other understanding that it is people who drive results in business, this new perspective was to have far-reaching ramifications.

My aim from then on has been to bring people to the heart of any business. People need to know they matter and they need to have a sense of belonging and to feel part of something bigger than themselves.

Using Robbins' 'six human needs' in the workplace

'GERONIMO'

As already mentioned (see 'Lived lessons in leadership' on the facing page) I developed a fascination with the work of Tony Robbins at the same time as I was returning to an area leader role and taking on 'Geronimo' which, at the time, was Flight Centre's globally most underperforming area. The area was comprised of eighteen stores across the north and west of Melbourne, of which only one was profitable. The other seventeen stores were all losing money. When comparisons were made, they showed that the poor results were not consistent with what was happening in other regions around the globe.

All of the KPIs that mattered were well below where they needed to be – sales results were poor, customer complaints were high, store brand standards were inconsistent, and retention was considerably lower than in other areas across Victoria. I needed to understand what was causing the area's disastrous results.

Spending time in stores, enabled me to witness the low morale first-hand. It appeared that people were on a kind of metaphorical hamster wheel. They were coming to work, selling some travel, going home, coming back the next day, selling travel, going home, and so on – day after day! There was no passion or enthusiasm, no shared goals, and no sense of community, which didn't make sense to me when what we sold was a wonderful life-changing product like travel, to customers who were generally very excited when they came into a store to plan and book a holiday.

I had coffee catch-ups with all eighty-four people working in the area. Feedback from team members was consistent. The more they shared about how they were feeling made it obvious to me that what they were saying was consistent with Tony Robbins' 'six core human needs'. What those people were missing in their workplaces was:

- certainty
- variety
- significance
- connection
- growth
- contribution.

I could link every problem they expressed to one of the 'six human needs' that wasn't being met.

I sought and gained access to several exit interviews conducted with people who had recently left the area. I found that I could link each reason given for leaving with a need from Robbins' six that wasn't being met.

Some of the key reasons for people leaving are included in the table on the next page.

WHY PEOPLE LEAVE	
REASON FOR LEAVING	THE NEED THAT WASN'T MET
Rosters being confirmed and communicated at the last minute	Certainty
Bored with the current role and needed a change of role or environment	Variety
Didn't feel valued or appreciated	Significance
Didn't get along with the store manager	Connection
Lack of training, development and career opportunities	Growth
No autonomy to make decisions relevant to their role	Contribution

Turnover of travel consultants was high, often meaning stores were left with people who had only limited experience and product knowledge. Recruiting and training of a new person was estimated to cost $40,000. With turnover so high, this became very costly.

It became evident to me that strategically finding ways to meet each of the 'six human needs' would mean that people would stay with our business longer, build their knowledge, increase their customer base, and have a bright future, with the ability to move into leadership roles if they desired. This would represent a key strategy for improving retention and would ultimately improve results.

When people's human needs are met, they stay longer and perform better. After three years in my role as the area leader of 'Geronimo', this strategy resulted in the area growing from eighteen stores to twenty-three stores and becoming the second most profitable area globally.

Your people are humans first and employees second.

'VICMANIA'

From my success with improving results significantly in the region known as 'Geronimo', by applying strategies aimed at fulfilling Robbins' 'six human needs', I knew that there were lessons to be learned from using that approach to improve performance at every business level.

When I became the leader of 'VicMania' (Victoria/Tasmania), I faced similar challenges to those I had experienced in 'Geronimo', but on a much larger scale – leading 142 stores.

I applied a similar approach to the one I had used previously – beginning by speaking to all area leaders and several store managers, and reading plenty of exit interviews. Once again, I could identify that people were unhappy or leaving the business altogether because their needs were not met.

Of course, the people I spoke with did not use Robbins' language. For example, if someone left because they didn't feel valued or appreciated; they would not have said that their 'need for significance was not being met'. But the connections were not difficult for me to make.

I then spent considerable time teaching area leaders and support leaders about Robbins' 'six core human needs', and together, we implemented strategies aimed at meeting people's needs within the business.

Key strategies

Some of the key strategies that were implemented to meet each of the 'six human needs' are listed in the table on the facing page.

I am convinced that the implementation of strategies aimed at fulfilling the 'six core human needs' was pivotal in turning the results around for both 'Geronimo' and 'Vicmania'.

The ultimate example for me of how the six core human needs can be fulfilled in the workplace came with the recognition 'Vicmania' received at Flight Centre's annual global gatherings, held specifically to recognise and acknowledge performance and achievement. To varying degrees, being recognised at that function, in front of their peers, also fulfilled or recognised the fulfilment for the 'Vicmania' team of all six of the core human needs ('certainty'; 'variety', 'significance', 'connection', 'growth' and 'contribution') – especially the needs for connection and significance.

KEY STRATEGIES	
NEED	**STRATEGIES FOR MEETING NEEDS**
Certainty	• Provide regular feedback on performance during one-on-ones and store visits. • Ensure rosters are done four weeks in advance. • Area leaders communicate their schedule of store visits in advance and have a structured approach to fulfilling them.
Variety	• Rotate responsibilities within stores. • Remove barriers preventing people from transferring to other stores/brands or moving into support roles.
Contribution	• Make the training of new team members the responsibility of everyone by implementing a 'buddy system'. • Encourage everyone to be involved in charities in a meaningful way, with the support of the business. • Always highlight the important work people do and the impact they have on the lives of customers.
Connection	• Hold quarterly off-site area leader planning retreats. • Hold monthly face-to-face region-based team leader meetings, facilitated by the area leader. • Encourage, and budget for, regular team gatherings.
Significance	• Hold monthly 'buzz nights' (see page 151) to recognise great performances by teams and individuals. • Acknowledge all the store team members by them having regular coffee catch-ups with area leaders. Store managers also have regular coffee catch-ups with senior leaders. • Always find ways to communicate appreciation and ensure that people feel valued for the work they do.
Growth	• Provide regular career planning for everyone in the business, from casual team members to senior operations and support leaders. • Provide regular training opportunities for everyone, related to their current role or future roles. • Focus on proactive succession planning and recruiting from within the business for support roles and senior roles.

Taking responsibility for retention

Regardless of their role, when someone leaves your business, you need to ask yourself, 'What need was not being met for them, influencing their decision to leave?' Not only will this help you think about strategies and actions that could be implemented or changed to help retain other people but it will also ensure that leaders take responsibility for providing an environment of which people want to be a part.

When people's needs are met, they stay longer, remain engaged, and perform their roles at a much higher level. When people are engaged, they will deliver better results for your business and for your customers.

Learning/appreciating the 'six core human needs' and implementing ways for them to be fulfilled is central to all my leadership training with retail leaders. It is in that aspect of the training when significant 'lightbulb moments' and increased appreciation and understanding seem to happen.

Why retention matters

The retail industry is one of Australia's largest employers and one of its most volatile. Many of the retailers I have worked with say that their annual turnover figures are between 40% and 60%.

The cost of losing a junior casual team member in the retail industry in Australia can be significant. It includes various factors, such as lost productivity, as well as the cost of advertising the job, recruitment, onboarding and training of a replacement.

Studies show that the total cost of losing and replacing a team member can amount to a sum up to twice the annual salary paid for their role.[9] There are also other intangible costs, such as loss of engagement and cultural impact within the whole team due to one of the team members leaving.

While a whole raft of issues might cause an individual to leave a job, the retail industry turnover rate being so high suggests issues with the way retail roles are set up and with the kinds of people attracted to them.

---

9   Bersin, J., 17 August 2013, "Employee retention now a big issue: Why the tide has turned', *LinkedIn*, viewed 4 August 2024. <https://www.linkedin.com/pulse/20130816200159-131079-employee-retention-now-a-big-issue-why-the-tide-has-turned>.

Retailers I have worked with estimate that, from their experience, between 50% and 70% of all retail roles are part-time or casual. This means the roles are often given to people who can't work full-time, such as students, working parents, or people who need full-time work but are either underemployed or working several jobs.

The roles in retail are almost set up to churn through people.

Students leave their retail jobs because they need time to study, or their class schedules and work schedules don't align.

The make-up of the retail workforce lends itself to high turnover, meaning retailers must better understand their talent pool before attempting to influence turnover rates. Rather than just accepting 'retail has high turnover', you may find you have enormous talent in your stores that just needs tapping into. Many senior leaders didn't plan for a long-term retail career but have managed to be very successful.

Losing senior leaders

Many middle managers and senior leaders leave retail businesses to take on a more senior role with a retail competitor. Typically, state and national managers have an increased appetite for personal growth, which is what has already driven them to reach the position they have in their careers.

Aside from the cost of the enormous amount of time and effort required to replace people who move on, there is also a risk of them taking key people with them. Often, this results from a lack of career conversations being had with their current leader, and those leaders not understanding people's hopes and desires and not having been able to plan a path to future roles for them. I have had many conversations with general managers and brand leaders about a person of great value who was about to leave when no one saw it coming. Efforts have been made too late to retain them, including offers of higher pay or responsibility, or attempts to convince them of a bright future if they stayed. Too often, the horse has already bolted.

Succession planning must happen regularly for everyone at all levels in the business and must be facilitated by the operational leader and not by the human resources team.

> ## Case Study: **Vanessa and Stacey**
>
> Vanessa, an area leader in Sydney, conducted an exit interview with Stacey, a casual team member who had resigned. Vanessa discovered that Stacey was leaving because she was relocating to regional New South Wales to study.
>
> Stacey was a good, reliable performer and Vanessa recognised that it would have been a shame to lose her from the business. Working with the regional area leader, Vanessa was able to arrange a transfer to a store located in the region to which Stacey was relocating. The transfer represented a win/win situation, filling an urgent vacancy in the region of Stacey's relocation and removing the stress for Stacey of needing to find a new job.
>
> Stacey had been unaware that a transfer within her brand was even an option for her as she had rarely spoken to her area leader during her time in the business.
>
> If Vanessa had not conducted the exit interview herself, she would not have known Stacey's circumstances and reasons for leaving, so a valued team member would have been lost.
>
> Not only did Stacey relocate but she was also promoted to an assistant manager role in her new store, providing her with more certainty and more income.

Exit interviews

An exit interview is aimed at uncovering why people leave. However, for many retailers, these interviews become no more than a box-ticking exercise.

Exit interviews are one of the most valuable, yet under-utilised, sources of information to which business leaders have access. While the human resources people are often the gatekeepers of this information, business leaders must have timely access to it and need to be able to use it to guide their business strategy.

How are you using the information from your exit interviews?

Case Study: **Pamela and Michael**

Pamela, the area leader of a large restaurant chain, conducted an exit interview with Michael, a casual team member who had resigned. Pamela discovered that Michael's roster constantly had him working on Mondays and Tuesdays, which conflicted with his study schedule. As a result, he had no choice but to cancel the shifts he was rostered to work on those days.

The cancelled shifts caused the restaurant manager a lot of frustration and Michael was perceived as 'unreliable'. Michael was equally frustrated because, due to constantly declining or cancelling shifts and being seen as unreliable, he wasn't being given enough work during times when he wasn't at university and was available to work. As much as Michael loved his job, he wasn't getting enough hours and needed to find another job that would work with his studies.

As a result of Pamela conducting an exit interview, Michael's roster was amended to accommodate his studies, meaning he remained with the business.

The restaurant chain needed to address the significantly high turnover of casual team members it had been experiencing. As a result of Pamela having recognised Michael's problem, the general manager and the team of area leaders initiated a project in which all casual team members completed a questionnaire to help their leaders better understand their availability. As a result, the approach to rostering changed and included the rostering of people based on their 'ideal' availability. Rosters were also completed two weeks in advance.

Completing rosters was no longer the responsibility of area leaders but became the responsibility of the individual restaurant managers, who had a greater understanding of their team members and were better equipped to make changes to accommodate those people.

It was also made clear to the casual team members that the business would do its best to accommodate their availability but, with that effort being made, it was requested that they would bear that in mind, attempting to fulfil their shift obligations and not cancelling shifts.

The feedback from the casual team was overwhelmingly positive. They felt valued and heard.

Over the following three months, results were monitored. Cancellation of shifts decreased substantially, and retention improved by more than 40%.

The situations described in the preceding Case Studies about Vanessa and Stacey, and Pamela and Michael, represent just the tip of the retention iceberg.

THE EXIT INTERVIEW PROCESS

Once a person leaves a business, it is usual that someone working in payroll or human resources sends them a link so they can complete the exit process requirements. The problem is that the former team member rarely completes information requested in that process and, on occasions when they do, the information is rarely passed on to the operational leaders who could use it to influence changes for improving retention.

The following pitfalls are often evident in the way exit interviews are conducted.

- Exit interviews are not valued or referred to when building strategy; so, those in charge of operations pay little attention to them.
- Exit interviews are usually done using an online questionnaire, which doesn't allow feedback to be put into context.
- Exit interviews are the result of an ad-hoc process carried out by the people in payroll or human resources and the information they contain is not relayed to the people in charge of operations. Often, operational leaders do not even request to receive the information from exit interviews.
- The requests for the completion of exit interviews are sent out too late, usually days after someone has resigned. By this stage, the person leaving has 'checked out' and doesn't want to provide feedback – they have already 'moved on'.
- Exit interview feedback (when the business has been lucky enough to receive some) is retained by the human resources team, who are not the people who can really influence changes to the reasons why people leave.

MAKE EXIT INTERVIEWS A CRUCIAL PART OF YOUR RETENTION STRATEGY

Exit interviews, when done well, should form a crucial part of your retention strategy. They uncover valuable information about specific stores and include information that can guide changes in strategy across the whole retail business.

What I have learned from my experience with exit interviews is that many of the reasons people give for leaving are very solvable and avoidable.

When working with area leaders, state managers and brand leaders, I spend considerable time helping them understand the value of exit interviews and why they must access the information provided in them. I even go as far as saying that area leaders should conduct exit interviews themselves so they can put in context the reasons why someone is leaving and, when necessary, take action.

When leaders have taken my advice and implemented the use of exit interviews as part of their retention strategy, they have been amazed not only at what they have learned about the reasons people are leaving but also at how they have been able to sort out some of the issues for particular people, to prevent them from leaving. Many have made positive inroads to retaining those people.

I am often baffled by how an inability to fix issues that are fixable can result in people needing to resign.

The Case Studies in this chapter highlight how several related issues can often be uncovered by conducting exit interviews. For example, an exit interview might reveal issues with:

- the way rosters are decided in stores
- who completes the rosters, and how far in advance they are communicated to the team
- the conversations store managers are having, or should be having, with their teams
- the ease, or otherwise, with which team members can move between stores
- the ease, or otherwise, with which team members can move between brands if the business is a retailer marketing multiple brands.

Everyone at an operational level, from store managers to national managers, general managers and CEOs, must appreciate that exit interviews are crucial components of a retention strategy.

To ensure exit interviews are conducted and the information they elicit is used as it needs to be, the exit interviews should be the responsibility of those in charge of operations, not the responsibility of the human resources team.

Ideally, exit interviews should become the responsibility of the area leaders, with information collated at a region, state or brand level to determine the reasons why people are leaving and what, if anything, can be done about those reasons.

If the completion of exit interviews continues to be the responsibility of the human resources team, once those interviews are completed, area leaders must have access to the information they contain. General managers and brand leaders need to read exit interviews related to their brand, so they can identify patterns emerging in the reasons why people leave.

The information from exit interviews should be discussed during area leader one-on-ones and monthly planning sessions (refer to Chapter 5, 'Alignment with goals and plans').

QUESTIONS FOR REFLECTING ON EXIT INTERVIEWS

Having accessed information from the exit interviews and observed patterns in that information, leaders will be in a position to answer these questions:

- Are there patterns consistent across exit interviews from this store/ area/brand?
- Is this something that needs attention?
- Does the information uncover a training opportunity or a necessary change in a system or process?

Tips for team retention

Each business will obviously be slightly different, but I know that a business in any industry will struggle to achieve its financial goals if it doesn't retain its best people. So knowing what it takes to keep great people is paramount.

Referring back to Robbins' 'six core human needs', the following are some suggestions for strategies to improve team retention.

1   Use gatherings, such as conferences and Christmas parties, along with other similar opportunities, as platforms for recognising your team members' achievements (results) and great performances. (Recognition of this kind fulfils the 'human needs' of 'significance' and 'contribution'.)

2   Encourage store managers and area leaders to thank their teams for their hard work. (Expressions of gratitude also fulfil the 'human needs' of 'significance' and 'contribution'.) You might assume this happens already, but my research into reasons for leaving as they were expressed in exit interviews says otherwise.

3   Your best team members and future senior leaders usually have an appetite for growth. Ensure you offer and provide training and development opportunities (fulfilling the 'human need' of 'growth'). The training offered doesn't need to be formal training; the opportunity to be mentored by senior leaders can also have a huge impact. Make career planning an important part of your people strategy.

4   Research has consistently shown that people stay or leave due to their relationship with their leader. Encourage team bonding with inexpensive group activities to help build strong relationships (fulfilling the 'human need' of 'connection').

5   Make feedback count. Senior leaders should use their store visits to receive feedback about the brand, how it can be improved, or regarding systems and processes that are difficult or unproductive. Some of the best ideas usually come from area leaders or front-line team members. (This fulfils their 'human needs' of 'significance' and 'contribution'.)

My experience has always led me back to considerations of how the people who work for a business feel about the ways in which that business meets their needs. Remember that your people are not motivated to come to work by the work; they come to work to meet their needs.

Light bulbs

Actions

Part 3:
Building your
strategy

Chapter 5

Alignment with goals and plans

Lived lessons in leadership

Preparing for a new financial year was always exciting – setting the budget and then looking at what each area should achieve and contribute to the overall numbers.

As part of the planning for the new financial year, I would sit down with each area leader. They would each be given their budget growth expectations for the new year and would look at each of their store's KPIs and provide feedback regarding which stores were likely to maintain constant results, which stores would increase their results marginally, and which could increase them significantly. Not only did this process improve the area leaders' business acumen but it also provided a level of ownership of the performance indicators – and a level of accountability. Understanding their area numbers and the individual breakdowns of each of the store's numbers enabled the area leaders to share the budget details with each of their store managers (see pages 87–8), so they could all work together on ways to achieve the desired results.

This process also shifted the mindset, from focusing on individual results to being across their region's overall KPIs. One-on-ones mirrored this mindset with focus being on the overall result as well as on individual store results.

The budgeting process is usually completed by the finance team, applying a growth percentage calculation, but from the process I undertook it became clear that, while the finance team play an important role in the budgeting process, it will be the operational team who are accountable for delivering the necessary numbers. If they are to be the accountable ones, it is essential that the people of the operational team understand the numbers and have ownership of them.

What are 'silos' across teams, and why should we avoid them?

If you have even been driving in agricultural grain-growing areas in the country, you will probably have seen individual silos used to store harvested grain.

In the context of leadership teams and structures, I use the term 'silo' as a metaphor to refer to different divisions, or those in different support roles, operating in isolation from one another, rather than collaborating and sharing information effectively.

Within a leadership team, 'silos' can manifest when the members of each support team become focused solely on their own goals and priorities without considering the broader strategic goals of the business.

What happens when 'silos' exist?

'Silos' can be very damaging and costly to a business.

Can you identify any frustrations you experience in your business because of individuals who provide different functions within different disciplines operating in separate 'silos'? Is the marketing team doing one thing, while the product or merchandising team is doing something else?

Regardless of the size of your business, it is crucial to have all parts of the business 'on the same page' and to have everyone aligned to the same vision, goals, and strategies.

Creating alignment and avoiding 'silos' helps with efficient decision-making. Reaching agreement regarding decisions becomes easier when everyone has been involved in formulating the strategy and knows and understands where the business is heading.

In businesses, I often see 'silos' develop between the operations team and the human resources team. The human resources team might work hard to contribute to good business outcomes and show enormous commitment to supporting the business, but I often begin to question who is leading who. Does the human resources team work to support the operations team? Are operations team members abdicating responsibility and leaving it to the human resources team to solve problems that really should rest with operations? For example, I have worked with retailers whose exit interviews are facilitated by the human resources team, with area leaders (sometimes for privacy reasons) prevented from accessing crucial feedback from those interviews even though the information relates to what is happening in their stores. At the same time, the area leaders might not even be requesting that information to help them formulate strategies to address issues.

As was discussed in the previous chapter, exit interviews collect data that should be considered as valuable information and could be used to assist with implementing strategies for reducing 'people-related issues' and improving retention. The only people who can improve retention are the operational leaders, but nothing will change if they are unable to access or refer to necessary information, like the feedback gathered from exit interviews.

I have worked with numerous human resources and 'learning and development' teams. Without doubt these teams of people work hard to support and contribute to businesses but, as well-intended as they may be, they are often working in a 'silo'.

I often say to area leaders, 'People from human resources are not awake at 3:00am worrying about issues in your stores.' Store issues remain problems for the operational leaders to solve – but the human resources team represents an invaluable resource for helping to solve them.

This separation and lack of connection is not necessarily the fault of the people involved. If they have not been given direction or been involved in creating strategy, they will make decisions based on what they think is best for the business. The operations team and the human resources team play vital roles but must work together and be aligned to the same goals and strategy.

The need for alignment

For a business to sustain growth, everyone involved in operations, product development, marketing and merchandising must be aligned to the same strategy. Rather than operating in 'silos' and making decisions based solely on what is best for the function they perform, everyone should collaborate and ask, 'What decision should we make to move us all closer to achieving our brand's goals?' When there is alignment across all operational teams, it becomes so much easier to make business decisions.

Different retailers can be at different stages of growth. Some retailers are working on a rapid growth and expansion plan, which might include opening more stores in new markets or relocating stores to bigger, more prominent sites. Alternatively, a retailer might have underperformed over time and could need to focus on turning around their results or improving results quickly.

A retailer might also be in maintenance mode, with good results meaning there are no plans to open more stores. That business might focus on looking for new growth strategies to sustain results.

Having everyone clear on the state of the business and where it is going will help determine your strategy and where you need to focus. This will also help decide what skills need to be prioritised across the team.

The goals you set should always be goals that will lead to financial success.

I do not intend sharing how to set goals, because many retailers already do this well and already understand that a plan is essential for guiding business growth and success. But the greatest challenge are:

- to create alignment across the business
- to keep the goals you set alive throughout a financial year
- to use your plan as a roadmap for success, without losing momentum.

Momentum can be lost because key people responsible for delivering various aspects of the plan leave the business. Loss of momentum can also be a symptom of results falling short of expectations and panic setting in, causing a well-thought-out plan to fall by the wayside.

The following text describes a system that I have experienced working very effectively. You can amend and adjust this suggested communication system depending on the size and structure of your business.

A system for achieving alignment across senior leadership teams

ANNUAL SENIOR LEADERSHIP PLANNING RETREAT

This retreat is held for at least two consecutive days annually, usually in the last quarter of the financial year, when it is a time for reflection on the past year and for developing goals, plans and high level budgets for the year ahead. It needs to be held at an off-site location, away from the day-to-day business environment.

Providing an opportunity for members of the senior leadership team to contribute to the plans for shaping the year ahead and ensuring financial goals are agreed upon, this retreat is also an invaluable opportunity for those in attendance to connect with the rest of the team across levels of seniority.

QUARTERLY SENIOR LEADERSHIP PLANNING DAYS

Those who attended the annual planning retreat should also attend quarterly planning days to ensure implementation, ownership and accountability for all goals and plans.

Quarterly planning days (ideally held off-site, for at least one day) are a time to bring your senior leadership team together to reflect on the past quarter. These days help to break down 'silos' that can exist when everyone isn't completely clear about the business goals and strategy. I prefer these to be held off-site to avoid the day-to-day business distractions and allow everyone to focus without interruption.

During these quarterly planning days, a great opportunity is provided to complete a SWOT analysis (**s**trengths, **w**eaknesses, **o**pportunities and **t**hreats; see pages 88–91), to assess how the business is tracking towards the goals and plans agreed upon at the annual planning retreat. Bringing the senior leadership team together quarterly ensures everyone continues to be aligned with the same goals and plans, and allows for adjustments to be made to any strategies if required.

Quarterly planning is often focused on strategy. However, quarterly planning days also provide invaluable opportunities to focus on the important aspects of the workplace environment, enabling the senior leadership team to enhance relationships, connections, and collaboration with others. Improving personal workplace relationships through that interaction can be very powerful.

The quarterly planning days also provide a fantastic opportunity to accelerate the senior team's leadership development by inviting industry experts to speak to the group on specific topics or to facilitate leadership workshops.

MONTHLY SENIOR LEADERSHIP TEAM MEETINGS

The senior leadership teams should meet between the quarterly planning days, at the end of each month. These meetings should focus mainly on operations but should follow the progress of the goals and plans to which everyone in attendance committed on the last quarterly planning day. This should include a focus on all aspects of delivering the different parts of the business strategy and on those who accepted responsibility for them.

Reflect on the month that has been and the month ahead and ensure that delivery of the strategy's requirements is on track for the quarterly goals to be achieved. Aside from helping to ensure everyone is still 'on the same page' and aligned to the same goals, these meetings provide an opportunity to raise and discuss challenges, especially if the month's results are less than expected. Whatever needs adjusting can then be addressed.

Elevating the role of state managers

Depending on the size and structure of your business, you may have state managers as well as area leaders.

A state manager's role can vary depending on the size of the business, but I often observe that the approach to the role can resemble that of an elevated area leader, especially if they have a very small area leader team or are responsible for stores themselves. State managers need to have a strategic and operational approach to their roles and should not need to micromanage or to just become highly paid area leaders.

If you can elevate the role by involving your state manager(s) in the formulation of business strategy and by having them attend retreats and quarterly planning days, they will be better able to lead their area leader teams more strategically. They will also be able to 'stay in their lane' (see pages 100–101) and allow their area leaders the independence to do their jobs.

QUARTERLY PLANNING RETREATS WITH AREA LEADERS

I strongly recommend that state managers (or whichever leaders to whom area leaders report) hold quarterly planning retreats with their area leaders and state-based support teams. These retreats should be held over two consecutive days, preferably away from the support office.

I do appreciate that your reactions to the suggestion of holding quarterly retreats might include, 'We don't have a budget to cover quarterly planning retreats,' or 'We can't afford for area leaders to be away from the business for two days each quarter.' These reactions are understandable, but I have always believed prevention is better than cure. I have worked with over 500 area leaders over recent years, many of whom were in need of more clarity, direction and connection – which quarterly planning retreats would have provided.

The value of investing in quarterly planning days with area leaders needs to be recognised. It will alleviate many issues of clarity, direction and connection, and will reduce the challenges with which their leaders are often left to deal.

Even if this strategy requires area leaders to all fly to one central location, I believe this would be money well spent.

Area leaders need to understand 'the big picture' but, more importantly, they must be clear about what needs to be implemented. Having state managers involved in senior leadership planning makes it easier for them to share strategy and plans with their area leader teams.

State-based quarterly planning retreats allow area leaders to review their results from the previous quarter and align their actions with the goals for the quarter ahead. It's a great opportunity for area leaders who are achieving great results to share their strategies with the rest of the area leaders so they can learn from each other.

The planning retreats also allow area leaders to be connected and build strong relationships. Area leaders are often very reactive, but these planning retreats enable them to take a more proactive approach to the role. The retreats also help hold area leaders accountable for what they must deliver to meet expectations.

Admittedly, during the quarterly two-day retreats we usually did some great leadership development work together, but the most important benefit was that the area leaders were provided with an opportunity to connect and feel part of the bigger picture, which was critical in creating in them a strong sense of unity and belonging. It was an effective way to meet all six of the 'human needs' discussed in Chapter 4.

MONTHLY AREA LEADER PLANNING SESSIONS

The area leader team should meet between the quarterly planning days, at the end of each month. These meeting should be facilitated by the state manager or whoever the area leaders report to. The focus of the meetings needs to be the progress towards goals and plans, the results for the month that has been, and ensuring that every area leader is focused on the month ahead with clear goals and the strategies for achieving them.

These meetings provide an excellent opportunity for area leaders to learn from each other and solve challenges together. They also help fast-track the development of the area leaders.

Summarising this approach

The following table outlines the communication and planning methods I recommend for each level of leadership, to keep everyone aligned to the same set of goals and accountable for attaining them. As was said earlier, you can adjust these suggestions to suit your business's size and structure. Once alignment is achieved, everyone can get on with fulfilling their roles.

You might feel that the suggestions, aimed at people from different levels of leadership, seem a bit repetitive in places – but that's the point! This system means that your communication is streamlined and efficient and will ensure everyone is 'on the same page'. It eliminates the need for a lot of conversations that might have been required for 'putting out fires'.

ALIGNING GOALS AND PLANS ACROSS ALL LEVELS OF SENIOR LEADERSHIP			
LED BY	**TYPE OF COMMUNICATION**	**WHO ATTENDS**	**WHEN**
CEO/ General manager	**Annual senior leadership planning retreat** • Review the year and expected results. • Complete a full SWOT analysis. • Set the strategy for the year ahead.	The senior leadership team, brand leaders and state managers	Annually across two days during the last quarter of the financial year
	Quarterly senior leadership planning days • Review results for the quarter. • Realign and commit to the business strategy for the quarter ahead.	The senior leadership team, brand leaders and state managers	Quarterly, held for one day

LED BY	TYPE OF COMMUNICATION	WHO ATTENDS	WHEN
CEO/ General manager/ National manager/ Brand leader	**Monthly senior leadership team meetings** • Focus on operations. • Reflect on the past month. • Plan for the month ahead. • Track the progress/accountability of strategies decided upon at the quarterly planning retreat.	The senior leadership team, brand leaders and state managers	Held at the end of each month, except for months when quarterly planning days are scheduled
	Quarterly planning retreats with area leaders • Held off-site (preferably). • Review the results for the previous quarter. • Accountability for the strategy, and actions for the quarter ahead. • Build capability. • Create connection. • Recognise great results.	State manager, area leaders and state-based support leaders/ business partners	Quarterly
State manager	**Monthly area leader planning sessions** • Treat these as the most important days of each month to create focus and alignment for area leaders. • Held as close to the last day of each month as possible. • Review the month's area results. • Recognise great area results. • Gather updates from various support team members. • Realign everyone to the strategy and actions for the month ahead.	State manager, state-based area leaders and the state-based support team	Held at the end of each month, except for months when quarterly planning days are scheduled

Please also see page 194 for a summary of a similar approach for aligning the goals and plans of state leaders and area leaders.

Keeping your business plan alive

Here are some tips for keeping your business plan and strategies alive and relevant.

1 **Align everyone around a small number of priorities**

Decide what your most important priorities are for the next year . . . the next 90 days, etc. Having too many priorities creates confusion and causes a lack of focus.

2 **Review your business plan regularly**

Schedule regular times to review your business plan. This ensures that everyone stays focused on the goals, identifies areas for improvement, and enables any necessary tweaks or changes to be made.

3 **Measure your progress**

Your KPIs will track your progress toward your goals. This will help identify areas in which you are succeeding and those on which you need to focus. It will also help determine whether strategies for some parts of the business must be revisited and revised in planning sessions.

4 **Be flexible**

Be open to adapting the business plan to deal with changes in the market and within the business. Being open to change will help the business to stay relevant and competitive. But be careful not to panic and overreact; be clear on what you are measuring and whether it matters.

Some plans will deliver longer-term results, so you need to balance this against any short-term challenges and problems.

5 **Communicate your plan**

Share your high-level goals and plans with people at all levels of the business, especially your store teams and your casual team members (remember from my experience, they make up 50%–70% of your workforce, see page 63).

Recognise and celebrate milestones and successes along the way. This will help keep your team motivated and engaged in the plan.

6 **Keep the team involved**

Throughout this book I have attempted to emphasise that people are an essential part of a business's success. Keep your team members involved in business planning and encourage them to contribute their ideas and feedback.

For more on the importance of communication, see Chapter 12, 'A system for communicating'.

Giving 'ownership' to area leaders and store managers

Many retailers have very sophisticated reporting processes. Store sales results can often be seen in real-time across the business, but there is also a missed opportunity for area leaders and store managers to take more ownership of results.

For example, on day four (the last day) of my Ultimate Area Leader program, I highlight the need for area leaders to 'work *on* their business' (WOB) at the end of each month (as opposed to 'working *in* the business'). The time for this is allocated at the start of the month and it is time set aside to reflect on the previous month's results and to plan and prepare for the month ahead.

As part of teaching area leaders to 'WOB', I ask each one what their monthly area budget is. Often, a blank look is the response, followed by them needing to open their laptops to trawl through reports and gather the necessary information. They can easily locate each store's budget for that day, but their area's total monthly sales budget is a different story.

This may indicate these area leaders are working on day-to-day, store by store, results rather than recognising that, as a senior business leader for a community of stores, they need to be looking at results of the area as a whole as well as store by store. That still requires thinking about each store's budget – but it also requires a firm understanding of the bigger picture, which is that all those store-by-store results are components. Store managers need to appreciate that they contribute to something bigger than just their store results.

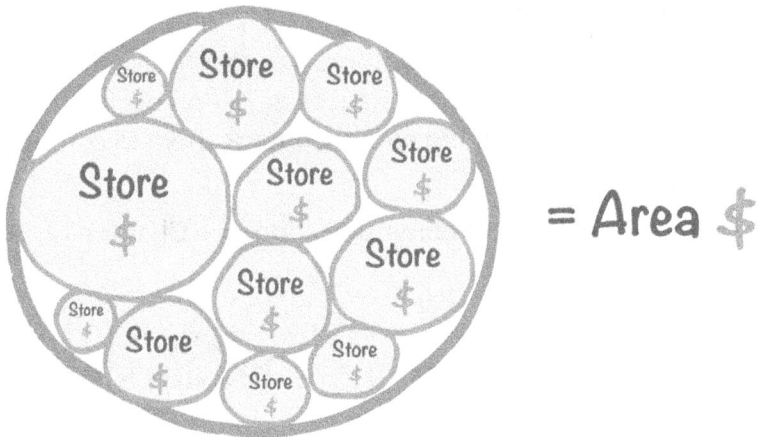

= Area $

When you create an environment in which people are part of a community and aligned to the same goals, they become more responsible and more motivated to achieve. Identify where you can inspire store teams to stretch their results, as well as which store teams may need to revise what they can achieve without waiting until the end of the month.

You can't change what you don't acknowledge. A review is particularly important midway through the month to assess overall results and identify which stores need to be inspired to stretch for more. Ultimately, area leaders are responsible for achieving their overall monthly region budget, but they often miss opportunities because they are only looking at their overall results at the end of the month (rather than throughout the month) and becoming demoralised when they fail to achieve the desired results.

To hold people accountable, be clear on expectations

The OAR for achieving team goals

When discussing the achievement of team goals, I like to use the acronym 'OAR' and refer to the sport of rowing:

A crew of rowers must work together to propel their boat efficiently through the water. Each rower must synchronise their movements with the rest of the crew to ensure that the oars simultaneously enter and exit the water. This is crucial for maintaining balance and maximising the power of each stroke. Communication helps the crew adjust their stroke rate, timing and technique in the manner needed to respond to the changes in conditions or strategy. Trust is crucial in a rowing crew. Each rower must trust that their teammates are doing their part and giving their best.

The point is that the members of a rowing crew can achieve their goals and perform at their best on the water by working together with coordination, communication, trust and adaptability.

The fitting acronym used for describing this, 'OAR' (**o**wnership, **a**ccountability and **r**esponsibility), can also be used to describe what is required in the context of leadership:

- **Ownership:** When someone takes ownership, they personally commit to the success or failure of whatever they are undertaking. This involves completing what is assigned to them, proactively addressing challenges and finding solutions.
- **Accountability:** This is the willingness to accept responsibility for one's actions and their outcomes. For leaders, it often involves being answerable for the results, whether they are successful or not. Accountability ensures that individuals are held responsible for their performance and deliver on their commitments.
- **Responsibility:** This involves the obligation to fulfil a role. It encompasses the actions and behaviours required to meet expectations and achieve outcomes. Responsibility involves understanding what needs to be done, making decisions and acting accordingly.

Accountability for results

Working with their state and national managers, area leaders should be involved in the full year, quarterly and monthly budgeting process for their areas.

Area leaders have the biggest influence on store results, so their involvement in the budgeting process is a crucial element of that process and also of growing their personal business acumen. Involving area leaders in the budgeting process can be one of your best opportunities to impact both your business and the area leader experience – but involving them might need to be a gradual process.

Although I will discuss incentives in Chapter 10, 'Reward and recognition', I will say here that, when area leaders take ownership of their results, they can also be held accountable for them and, therefore, responsible for the level of income they deserve.

Ensure support teams spend time in stores

Aside from the operational leaders, such as area leaders, state managers and general managers, people who usually work in different retail support offices (including finance, human resources, payroll, customer experience, product delivery and marketing) should spend some time in stores. These people are often responsible for making important decisions regarding systems and processes that directly impact the productivity of stores and their results.

I implemented structured quarterly store visits and referred to them as 'SWOT days' (days for reviewing and analysing **s**trengths, **w**eaknesses, **o**pportunities, and **t**hreats). These days provided an opportunity for all support leaders to spend time in stores and view store-based challenges and opportunities with fresh eyes.

The primary purpose of SWOT visits was for people who spent the majority of their time working in the support office to spend valuable time in stores. This would allow them to gather feedback to assist them in making informed and disciplined decisions. Without this structured approach, many support people would never spend time in stores, even though they were making crucial decisions that impacted store operations.

I found SWOT visits to be the best way to:

- build trust between the support offices and the stores
- provide feedback to stores regarding opportunities for improvement
- gather feedback from stores and to have a more empathetic understanding of their challenges

- structure a system for support teams to visit stores, to help make better informed decisions
- find opportunities for reducing red tape to enable stores to be more productive.

Setting up SWOT visits

A SWOT visit would happen in a single area once each quarter. This made it easier for feedback to be given to the area leader.

Senior support team leaders were paired together for the visits, meaning they also benefitted from spending time together collaboratively away from the support office.

The people at a store would be advised that a SWOT visit was occurring in their area so that they could think about and prepare any feedback they wanted to provide. Many retailers would prefer these visits to be unannounced, but I don't believe that makes the most of the opportunity and creates unnecessary anxiety in the store teams who are always nervous a visit will happen without warning.

Each pair of support leaders would visit a couple of stores to gather feedback. On occasions, there might be a particular focus derived from your business plan – such as ideas for team retention, or gathering feedback regarding a new system or process. Any feedback conversations needed to be a two-way process. They provided an opportunity for the leader from each type of support team to gather feedback related to their specific function within the business, as well as provide support, feedback and mentoring to the store teams.

Typically, the support leaders would take the store manager out for coffee and talk in-store to various team members who were working on the day of the visit.

After completing their store visits, the support team members would all meet at the support office and compare the feedback from the visits. That feedback was then collated and given to the area leader and state leader.

The information was used to assist with the development of the area leader and to guide the implementation of any opportunities for improvement that had been identified.

From my experience, area leaders found SWOT visits very useful. The visits represented a great opportunity for their areas to be examined with fresh eyes, and for them to hear positive and affirming feedback, or to be informed of suggestions for improving results.

THE STORE SWOT VISIT TEMPLATE

Well-intentioned systems and processes are often put in place to determine what is happening in stores, but they can often cause issues for the store teams by distracting them from their most important function – looking after customers.

These SWOT visits provide an invaluable opportunity for the support teams to gather feedback related to what they are doing well to support the store teams and what they could be doing better to support them and help them be more productive.

The visits also allow the support team to use their expertise to suggest ways each store they visit might improve its results and productivity.

Some people working in the more technical and isolated areas of the support team, such as finance, payroll, etc., may not be well-equipped to gather feedback in stores. It could be helpful to give them a structure to follow, to assist them to get the most out of their time in the stores.

On the next two pages there is an example of a template that might be useful, but I recommend creating your own template for your brand/business. You can adapt the template I have provided to suit the areas on which you want to focus. The template should be updated regularly based on the specific or seasonal/quarterly strategies on which you are focusing.

STORE SWOT VISIT TEMPLATE

STORE:_____ **DATE:**_____ **AREA LEADER:**_____

STORE PRESENTATION AND BRAND STANDARDS

Merchandising
Is stock merchandised correctly and well-presented?

Store front
Was the storefront clean, inviting and up-to-date?

Overall store presentation
Was the store clean and tidy?

Store environment
How did the store feel? Were you warmly greeted? Was the store welcoming?

Customer service
Were customers greeted in a timely manner and offered assistance?

Team presentation
Were team members well-presented and on brand?

Store goals
Are there clear goals towards which the store is working?

Are the goals known and understood by the team?

(Continued on next page)

(Continued from previous page.)

STORE PRESENTATION AND BRAND STANDARDS

Business systems (relevant to each support discipline)
Are the correct business systems in place?

Are there any systems or processes that stores find time-consuming or challenging?

Feedback from the store manager
What improvements to systems and processes would make the lives of the store team members easier and improve their results?

Feedback from the store team members
What would make lives of store team members easier and make their results better?

What else do the stores need to maximise performance?

Suggestions
What other suggestions/feedback can you give the team leader to assist in their business?

Summary and feedback to give to the area leader
From spending time in stores, what did you consider to be working well?

What could be improved?

Feedback for my team
What did I learn from visiting stores?

How can my team improve support for the stores?

Light bulbs

Actions

Chapter 6

Creating empowered leaders

Why you need empowered leaders

The need for empowered leaders has become more crucial than ever before. Outdated top-down hierarchical structures for decision-making no longer support the fast-paced retail environment. What is needed are leaders who can adapt to change swiftly.

When leaders feel empowered, team engagement increases and team members feel valued and motivated, often leading to better decision-making.

It is likely that empowered leaders will to stay longer in the business and feel invested in its success. They will want to build their career within the business rather than look for opportunities elsewhere.

Case Study: Dawn

I was working with the regional and state managers of an Australian national fashion retailer and was fascinated to hear there was a distinct difference between results from state to state. As I came to increasingly understand the business structure and get to know the different leadership styles of the leaders, I was able to discern what could have been causing the inconsistent results.

The results in Victoria were significantly lower than those for the other states. There was a noticeable difference in the kinds of problems they were facing when compared to the rest of the country. For example, Victoria had higher turnover of people and more 'people issues' in general, resulting in the human resources team often needing to step in to resolve them.

Interestingly, the business support office was based in Melbourne, Victoria.

Dawn, the state manager of Victoria, shared with me that she felt micromanaged, as if she was always being watched because, with her stores being located in Victoria, it was easier for the Victorian-based senior leaders and support people to visit them. She shared how her flagship store could receive up to three visits per week from various leaders in the business. She was constantly being 'advised' of the problems that existed in her stores. Dawn often felt deflated and constantly under the spotlight, which had impacted her confidence in making decisions.

Dawn also admitted that having easy access to the support team meant she would defer to them rather than making decisions for herself.

In states such as Queensland and Western Australia, where senior leaders weren't based and it wasn't all that easy for them to travel to often, the state managers felt more empowered and needed to make decisions for themselves. They just seemed to be able to get on with it and this was reflected in their positive results.

I sympathise when I hear stories from store managers working in a state where the support office is located. For some of the big 'flagship' stores, it is not unusual for area leaders, the state manager, the national manager and the general manager to make several store visits each month. Each leader has a say and provides observations and feedback about the store, regarding merchandising, store window displays and brand standards. Sometimes, feedback from different leaders can conflict, leaving store managers confused and unsure of themselves.

The store managers' one source of direction should be their area leader, whose source of direction is their state manager, and so on up the chain of leadership. If this is not the case, it can become very confusing and disempowering for the store managers, listening to input from too many voices.

Too much direction can also disempower the area leaders, preventing them from learning and growing. Undoubtedly, the results of the 'flagship' stores are crucial to overall results and demand the focus but, if you have your best store managers leading those stores, trust needs to be placed in their ability. Visits to those stores needs to be for a purpose aligned with two-way communication.

Despite this potential problem, people from all levels of leadership should still visit stores. Many of the people in support roles (such as finance, marketing, customer experience, human resources and payroll), who typically do not spend time in stores, should spend some time in stores. They should speak to the in-store teams to gain a better understanding of challenges and 'roadblocks' to store success, as well as the opportunities they could have to help provide support to stores. A lot can be learned from the people who are the best source of information – the store managers and their teams (see page 106).

Paying attention to behaviour will indicate to you the degree to which your leaders are empowered. The following table lists some signs of empowerment to reflect on in your own leadership behaviours and the behaviours of the leaders you lead.

DISEMPOWERED LEADERS VERSUS EMPOWERED LEADERS	
SIGNS OF DISEMPOWERED LEADERS	**SIGNS OF EMPOWERED LEADERS**
Appear unclear about long-term goals and work on the day-to-day.	Have clarity about their own roles and expectations. Can identify opportunities to achieve long-term goals.
Micromanage their teams, exhibiting a lack of trust in their people.	Build trust with their teams and work collaboratively regarding their decision-making and actions.
Speak to their own leaders often, seeking 'permission' to make decisions. May seek constant validation.	Can make reasonable autonomous decisions that they believe to be best for the business. Have the courage to take calculated risks.
Are given insufficient training and development opportunities to succeed in their roles.	Are given access to ongoing mentoring, and development to grow and perform in their roles.
Communication is in a 'tell' mode, rather than an 'ask' mode. They may fail to listen or gather feedback from their teams.	Are encouraged to put forward their own ideas for business improvement and foster a culture of collaboration and teamwork.
Feedback regarding performance is ad hoc and inconsistent.	Give feedback about exactly where their teams do well and where development opportunities lie.
Appear stagnant in their roles and don't demonstrate motivation to grow.	Are given opportunities for ongoing development, to grow personally and professionally.

(Continued on next page)

(Continued from previous page.)

SIGNS OF DISEMPOWERED LEADERS	SIGNS OF EMPOWERED LEADERS
Appear to show high levels of uncertainty when making decisions.	Can make decisions without fear of consequences.
Lose high calibre people who take on senior roles with other retailers.	Provide a career path for team members to work towards. Listen regularly to feedback offered by their teams regarding performance and environment.
Are not involved with or do not have ownership of the business strategy.	Have 'seats at the table' when business goals and strategy are being devised.
Don't offer opinions in team meetings for fear of 'getting it wrong'. May withhold information.	Are comfortable to put their ideas forward, regardless of whether the ideas are implemented or not.
Tend to wait for instructions rather than taking the initiative.	Will make decisions and back themselves, knowing that they will be supported even if the desired outcome isn't achieved.
Display a lack of creativity and innovation in problem-solving and may fear change.	Will try new strategies to solve problems and find solutions.
Work in a reactive way and focus on the day-to-day, with no forward planning or consideration of the bigger picture.	Create plans and use them as 'roadmaps' to work towards goals. Are adaptable and resilient in the face of change.
May be quick to shift blame onto others when things go wrong.	Take responsibility for their decisions and actions. Hold themselves, as well as others, accountable for achieving results.

Control versus influence

Control and influence are two related concepts, but the terms have different meanings:

- **'Control'** when used as a verb, refers to having power or authority over something or someone. It means being able to direct, manage, or regulate something to achieve a desired outcome.
- **'Influence'**, on the other hand, refers to the ability to affect or shape something or someone without necessarily exerting direct control over them. Influence can be used to persuade or convince someone to take a particular course of action.

One of the challenges with the leadership career path is that the higher in an organisation the leadership role you have attained the more *influence* you will have over the business strategy, but you will have less *control* over what happens day-to-day in stores and in whole areas of stores.

You will be reliant on state managers, area leaders, and store managers to do what needs to be done and ensure that what is meant to happen is happening. This is one of the biggest frustrations for senior retail leaders and often prevents them from letting go of control completely. However, the best senior retail leaders also recognise that micromanaging or trying to control everything rarely works.

So, how do you empower your teams of national leaders, state managers and area leaders to get the job done without you needing to personally control the day-to-day operations? How do you influence behaviour so that what is meant to happen does happen without you exerting too much control and limiting the autonomy of the leaders you lead? Your direct control will not be necessary if you are able to encourage and support the development of appropriate skills in the people you lead, provide them with direction and ensure everyone is on the same page.

Leaders at different levels of seniority in a business exert varying levels of control/influence on the people they lead, as shown in the diagram below.

Leadership styles necessary at different levels of seniority

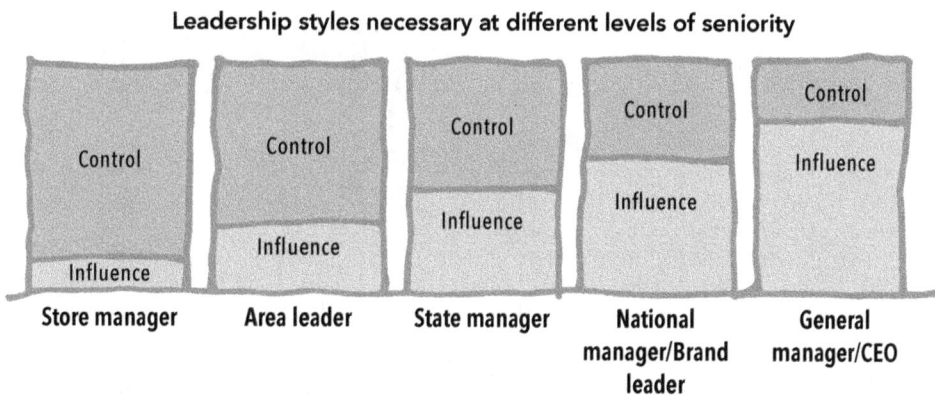

| Store manager | Area leader | State manager | National manager/Brand leader | General manager/CEO |

The further you go up the leadership ladder, the more influence you have over decisions and the direction of the brand, but the less control you have over implementing the business strategy. Understanding this, and preventing yourself from being caught 'in the brambles' of store operations, can be quite an adjustment.

Focus on your own role which is to:

- create direction
- align everyone to your vision, strategy, and goals
- set expectations
- manage expectations.

Through engagement and communication, you must align everyone in your team to a shared vision, goal and plan. While your focus needs to be on fulfilment of your own role, part of that role is ensuring that others fulfil theirs.

No one should be working in isolation. Different functions/divisions/areas must collaborate and share information effectively.

Stay in your lane!

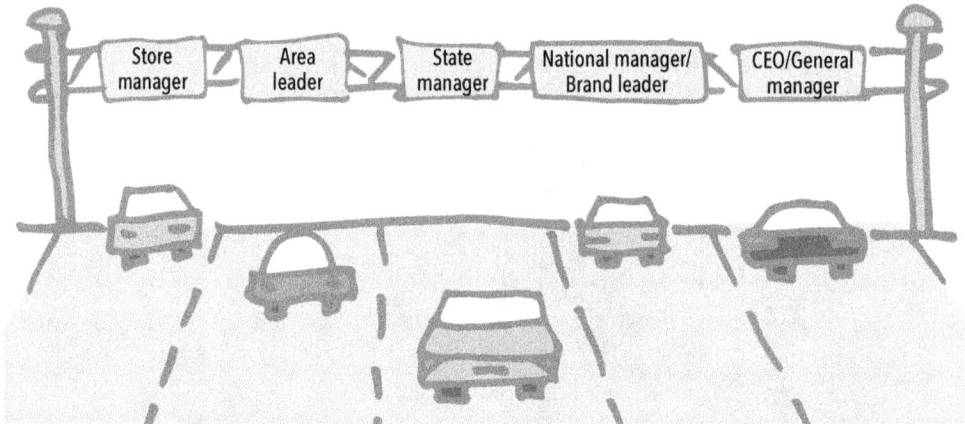

If leaders start to micromanage, they begin to take on part of the role that should be the responsibility of those they lead. The distinction between the roles becomes blurred and leaders begin doing jobs below their pay grade. This is not good economy.

- Are your area leaders acting as expensive store managers?
- Are your state managers acting as expensive area leaders?

I like to use the term 'stay in your lane' when attempting to help leaders understand that they should be doing their own job and not the job of someone who reports to them. This term is especially important to remember when results for which you are responsible are behind where they need to be. That is when pressure can mount, panic can set in and you can go off course, losing sight of the strategy and reverting to being controlling.

Remember, the further up the ladder you go, the less control you have. It can require a psychological adjustment to 'stay in your lane' as you progress from one senior role to another.

Leading when things aren't on track

Just like on the road, 'crashes' can happen in business when you don't stay in your lane. That usually occurs when you have felt the need to control, or to do the job that others in your team should have been doing.

If things aren't working, that should be the time to realign the team to the business goals and plan, and adjust anything that needs it (see Chapter 5, 'Alignment with goals and plans'). Most importantly, ensure everyone is connected, aligned with the plan, understands their role and is clear regarding expectations.

Avoid micromanaging

The more layers of leadership there are in your business, the more potential there is for micromanaging unless everyone has clearly defined roles. Micromanaging often occurs because your leaders and those they are leading are not clear on their roles and what is expected of them.

Once you are clear on each leader's responsibilities, set your expectations and then manage those expectations.

When assessing whether it is appropriate for you to address a situation directly with a team member, I like to use a 'bank account' metaphor, as explained on the next page.

The following 'bank statement' illustrates what I intend my banking metaphor to mean. Once you have had an opportunity for positive interactions ('Credits') with team members and have established yourself as more than a Level 1 leader with them (see John C. Maxwell's 'five levels of leadership' on pages 19–20), it is easier to raise matters regarding areas in which they could improve ('Debits') – rather than coming in cold with the constructive feedback from the outset before a relationship has been established between you.

R L B Retail Leaders Bank	Statement (Showing 6 transactions)	
Credit (all positive interactions)	Debit (constructive feedback)	Balance
+ Building trust		+
+ Praise		+ +
+ Positive feedback		+ + +
	— Have honest conversations	+ +
	— Address issues/concerns	+
	— Manage standards	0

Deposits   ↓ Withdrawals

Lived lessons in leadership

As a national leader at Flight Centre, whenever I visited a store it was primarily to spend time with the area leader as part of their development. It was also an opportunity to get to know the store manager – and to discuss their future career aspirations and offer advice. I always treated it as an opportunity to chat with the team, and gather feedback about what we could be doing, as a business, to provide more support to stores..

I recall visiting a store to have a one-on-one with an area leader. A new team member had just joined the team. It was his first day in the role after completing his novice training. The new team member was a lovely, personable guy. I had a brief chat with him about his experience during the training process and what he had done before joining us.

I then observed him assisting a client by providing a price for a holiday. He seemed to be doing a good job building rapport and was asking all the right questions. However, what I noticed next caused me to hyperventilate!

As part of the sales process, each client should receive a written quote, typed out professionally with all the details included, which makes it easier for a consultant to follow up and ensure all of the details of the enquiry are clear. It also makes it easier for the client to see what exactly is being recommended and included.

What I saw was the new team member writing the details of the quote on the back of his business card and giving that to the client. That was a big, big no-no! The correct procedure would have been covered thoroughly during his training, but he was not following it.

Now, while it would have been quicker and easier for me to address this break with accepted procedure directly with the new team member and explain why we do not do what he had just done, and why it didn't meet our customer experience standards, as his boss's, boss's boss I didn't feel that would be appropriate! I knew I needed to 'stay in my lane' and this needed to be dealt with by his leader.

This is where my 'bank account metaphor' comes in. I had no 'money in the bank' with that new team member. He had just met me for the first time, and it would have been completely intimidating and inappropriate for me to have addressed this with him. I hadn't 'deposited' anything into the relationship, so I had nothing to 'withdraw'.

During my one-on-one with the store's area leader I shared what I had observed. After that one-on-one discussion, she spoke with the young man's store manager who spoke with him to ensure the correct sales process was understood and was followed in the future.

The matter was still addressed quickly but the approach I took also allowed the store manager to take responsibility for the development of the team – which is part of the store manager's role.

When I said above that I hadn't 'deposited anything' I meant that, as far as that team member was concerned I was only a Level 1 leader to him (see John C. Maxwell's 'five levels of leadership' on pages 19–20). There had been no chance for me to gain his trust and establish a relationship, so anything I said to him could be intimidating purely because of my senior position in the business.

The best person to address that matter, teach the team member, and set future expectations for his performance was his store manager—and that was the course of action that was taken.

This is not to say that those of us in senior roles should ever turn a blind eye or let standards slip. There will be occasions when we need to address a situation immediately, but we also need to remember to 'stay in our lane' and support the development of the leaders we are leading by allowing them to address the issues that fall within their areas of responsibility.

As I have already highlighted, all retail leaders should spend time in stores. However, clarity regarding your purpose for store visits helps ensure that everyone does 'stay in their lane'. When senior leaders are in the stores, the purpose for the visits should be different from the area leaders' purposes for visiting stores.

Regardless of your actual role, the more senior your title and the further up the leadership ladder you are, the more intimidating it can be for the members of your store teams, especially casual team members. They won't necessarily be intimidated by you, but they undoubtedly can be intimidated by your title. You may be the boss of their boss's boss! It is important to consider this when providing feedback to stores.

It is crucial that you remain relatable and work to connect with your store teams. Be vulnerable; share the knowledge you have learned from your years of retail experience. Your journey through the ranks – the good, the bad, and the ugly of it – has got you to where you are now. It is important to remain relatable so your people can see that they too can achieve what you have achieved.

If there is positive feedback to acknowledge (positive sales results, as well as great customer feedback, merchandising, and store presentation), the time to deliver that praise is right away. There is no time like the present! People in stores love hearing positive things from the 'big bosses'.

However, if you need to offer 'constructive' feedback and point out areas requiring attention or improvement, it often proves to be a better learning experience for all involved if you coach your area leaders to deliver that feedback to stores rather than you delivering it directly. Just as positive feedback from very senior leaders can be inspiring and satisfying to hear, hearing feedback that is not so good directly from senior leaders can be destructive and demoralising. The responsibility of delivering that kind of feedback also offers a great development opportunity for area leaders.

The following table contains some examples of the purposes leaders in key roles could have for store visits. Use it as a model and take the opportunity to discuss the information it contains with your leadership team to devise your own similar table appropriate to your business structure.

PURPOSES FOR STORE VISITS		
ROLE	PURPOSE FOR VISITING STORES	ACTIONS
CEO	• To provide motivation and inspiration to stores. • To identify strategic opportunities. • To share the vision for the brand, and the brand's story.	• Spend time in stores talking to team members and store managers. • Schedule one-on-ones at a store with your direct reports.
National manager/Brand leader (or equivalent)	• Ensure brand standards are in place. • Ask for feedback about what is working and what extra help stores need to improve results. • Identify people suitable for future roles.	• Spend time in stores talking to the teams. • Have a one-on-one with the state manager/area leader to discuss their focuses, results and performance.
Support team members	• Get out of the support office and connect with store teams to build relationships. • Find ways to remove possible 'roadblocks' and red tape impeding store success.	• Gain feedback specific to your function from the store teams. • Gain an understanding of the 'roadblocks' to success faced by store teams. • Gain feedback related to each store team's level of support.
State manager (or equivalent)	• Meet with the area leader to provide development and feedback. • Ensure brand standards are in place. • Identify future leaders.	• Spend time in stores talking to the teams. • Have one-on-ones with the area leader. Discuss each of their stores' performance. • Get to know the future aspirations of the store managers and teams.

Tips for building an empowered leadership team

The following tips are intended to assist you to empower leaders at every level of your leadership team to be the best they can be.

1 Ensure everyone in the team understands the business vision, goals, and strategy and that everyone is aligned with them. (Refer to Chapter 5, 'Alignment with goals and plans'.)

2 Encourage your team members to share their ideas for continuously improving their processes. This isn't about 'getting it right' but about putting ideas on the table for discussion.

3 Provide regular opportunities for sharing what's working and what's not working across the brand. Make it 'safe' for your team members to offer feedback regarding a variety of support functions, especially if their views differ from your own. Make changes as necessary, so that you are validating their feedback when it proves useful.

4 Create an environment in which it's 'safe' to question why things are done the way they are and to offer suggestions for improving them.

5 Use store visits to gather feedback and remove roadblocks to success.

Based on how empowered you believe your team currently is, consider changes you might need to make to ensure you are leading in a way that sets clear expectations and then allows everyone to get on with what they are responsible for and to meet expectations.

What methods could you use to gather feedback so your leaders feel empowered and not micromanaged?

What shifts in mindset might you and your senior leaders need to make?

Light bulbs

Actions

Chapter 7

Empowerment and 'ownership'

Having a birds-eye view of various retailers, I am often asked what it is that sets the retailers who are doing well apart from those who are underperforming. I can say, without hesitation, that the results successful retailers are achieving are in direct proportion to the increased level of autonomy the leaders at all levels of their business have when making decisions. This includes store managers, area leaders, state managers, and national managers/brand leaders.

The impact of inefficiency and red tape might not be obvious – and neither will be the opportunities missed due to leaders being restricted in the kinds of decisions they can make without going up the chain of leadership for approval.

There is always room to expand the kinds of decisions, aligning with their roles and responsibilities, each leader can make. Encourage everyone to 'level up' and' stay in their lane' rather than take on responsibility for roles further down the leadership chain.

If the members of your team are taking ownership of their roles and results, it is likely that they also have sufficient autonomy to make the decisions necessary to achieve those results. On the other hand, if you consider your team members to have a low rating when it comes to taking ownership of their roles and results, it is very likely that they also have little autonomy when it comes to making decisions to achieve results.

The graph on the next page is a stylised representation of the interdependent way responsibility and autonomy affect performance and the ownership that team members have of results.

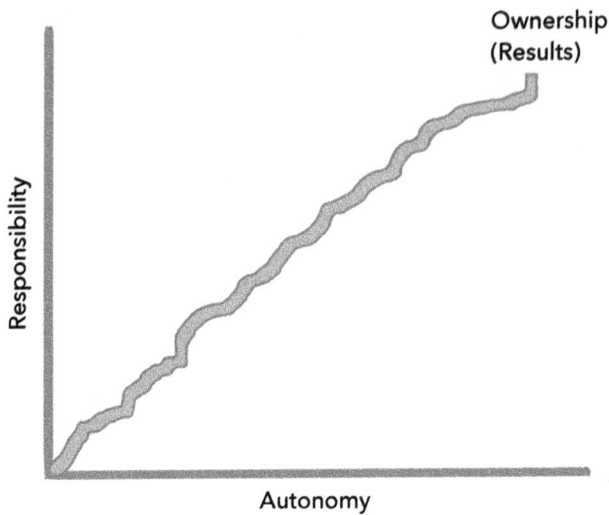

If you are frustrated that leaders do not take the amount of responsibility you would like them to take, you need to ask yourself whether that lack of responsibility is a result of them not being given a level of autonomy that would allow them to take ownership of outcomes and results.

Case Study: **Moira**

Moira was a very experienced store manager at a popular direct factory outlet. It was a busy afternoon and by 2:30 pm the store was on track to hit budget.

With a store full of customers, Moira could see there was an enormous opportunity to finish the day strongly, however her casual team member, Kylie, was due to finish her shift at 3:00 pm.

Kylie would have been happy to stay longer, but Moira was not authorised to make the decision to extend her shift. Moira called her area leader and explained the opportunity and that, considering the store was behind budget for the week, she was motivated to finish the day strongly.

Her area leader advised that she wasn't authorised to extend Kylie's shift. She would need to check with her state manager to authorise the extension of Kylie's shift by one hour and would get back to Moira after that.

A little while later, Moira received a call to say that it would be okay for Kylie to work later but, by that time, Kylie had already finished her shift and left the store at 3:00 pm.

Moira was totally frustrated. She had been fearful that, if she had asked Kylie to stay beyond the time of her designated shift, she would get into trouble. She was also frustrated that she wasn't trusted enough to make a decision that could have made the store money and enabled her to exceed her budget.

If we were to calculate the cost of that lost opportunity with the accumulated cost of Moira (the store manager) calling her area manager, who then called her state manager – along with the cost of lost productivity and sales – the total would have been more than the additional wages required for Kylie, the casual team member, to have stayed for an additional hour.

Leaders who are enabled to make important business decisions relevant to their role are able to gain a greater psychological and 'spiritual' ownership of the business and their results.

I am sometimes amazed that many well-paid senior leaders are not given the autonomy to make decisions I would consider it reasonable for them to make based on their position in the business. Moira, the store manager in the situation described in this Case Study, had been the store manager for several years and was well regarded in the business. She knew what was needed but was unauthorised to act on that decision without approval from her leader's leader.

Working with many retailers, I have seen that there is an enormous opportunity for area leaders and store managers to make more decisions than they currently do. Not only would increasing their ability to make decisions lead to them having more spiritual ownership of their roles, the business and results, but it would also often lead to decisions being made in a better, more timely manner. It would also make leaders more accountable for their results.

The more ownership of their overall area sales budget we can develop and encourage in area leaders – and the more we can hold them accountable for meeting that budget – the more empowered those leaders will feel. Holding people accountable for their results is only possible if they are given reasonable autonomy to make decisions that they believe will positively impact their expected results. It is important to note that not every decision a leader makes will be the right one. Mistakes will always be made. However, it is easier for a leader to own a mistake when they can also own the decision that led to it.

Why empowerment matters

When leaders don't feel they are able to make decisions, they relinquish responsibility – not because they want to but because they fear making mistakes and dealing with the consequences of those mistakes.

If your team has leaders with a need for growth (refer to Tony Robbins' 'six core human needs' on page 55), you should thank your lucky stars because those leaders will be open to new ideas, strive to find solutions, and love being challenged.

On the flip side, if you have leaders with a high need for growth who feel micromanaged, they will stagnate once their need for growth can no longer be met. It is likely that they will leave the business and look to meet that need for growth elsewhere.

The reality is that most great leaders have a high need for growth – which is great for the business if they are given the chance to develop, but it is frustrating for them if the business cannot meet that need.

I have observed many outstanding retail leaders with a high need for growth who have left their roles to work for another retailer because they were unable to meet their need for growth within their former business. It is a great shame if senior business leaders have invested time and effort into the development of those retail leaders but haven't been able to 'loosen the rope' to empower them so they can continue to grow and progress.

Innovation versus the possibility of failure

Fear of failure can be a roadblock to trying new strategies. You need to ask yourself:

- how significant your appetite for innovation is
- how significant your fear of failure is.

These are decisions that need to be made about the culture of the business.

To have a culture of innovation, you must accept that not every new idea or initiative will succeed. But, for example, if you look to implement five new ideas of which two work while three fail, that is progress and should be celebrated. Even the failures can be learning opportunities and, hopefully, the two ideas that worked will make a significant positive difference to the business. It is better to have two new strategies that work and are having a positive impact on the business than to have none at all, and the only way to know what does work is to remain open to trying new strategies.

When you don't allow leaders to make decisions, the opportunity for great innovation can often be missed. What if leaders' fear of failure meant there was no point in raising an idea or acting on an opportunity to improve the business? In that case, everyone would keep doing what they have always done, even if they believed that what they were doing was making no difference to results.

When decision-making (of even the most basic kind) requires the involvement of multiple people, everything takes longer to implement. Having a culture of empowerment must start at the top, and senior leaders must lead by example when it comes to empowering those they lead.

Have clear expectations and manage them

Whenever I begin to work with a retailer, I usually commence by working with the senior leaders of the business. The topics of 'autonomy' and 'ownership' are key.

I ask a series of questions to understand the level of autonomy that exists for each of the leadership roles within the business. I try to determine what is expected of the people in those roles and how well those expectations are communicated to them.

Having gained some understanding regarding ownership and autonomy from the senior leaders is particularly important when, after working with them, I begin to work with the area leaders. I want to ensure that I am not teaching the area leaders strategies they will not be allowed to implement, because that would just be setting them up to fail.

It is in regard to the level of autonomy area leaders actually have that the greatest variation of perception lies. The belief and expectation senior retail leaders have that their area leaders are empowered to make decisions is often totally disconnected from the actual circumstance. The contrasting perception of the area leaders themselves appears to be that they are very limited in what they can and can't make decisions about within the stores in their area. Many have commented during training with me: 'We would never be allowed to do that!'

After area leaders complete the training I provide, those who lead them are quite surprised when I quote feedback that the area leaders are unclear regarding their boundaries.

This highlights an opportunity to be clear about what decisions leaders can and can't make. Have their boundaries and degree of autonomy been communicated to the area leaders? Is there any confusion that needs to be clarified so that every state manager, area leader, store manager, and team member is clear on their role and their boundaries?

More importantly, are you disempowering your leaders by not allowing them to make more decisions than they currently do? Is this contributing to a culture that does not support innovation?

This topic will be a great conversation starter across your senior leadership team. An open discussion of this topic can result in their being more certainty of a correlation between the decisions senior leaders perceive and expect to be made by those they lead and the decisions that are actually being made further down the chain of leadership.

A table similar to the one below could assist with recording and defining the decision-making roles so everyone is clear.

RETHINKING DECISION-MAKING ROLES	
ROLE	DECISIONS THAT SHOULD BE MADE AT THIS LEVEL THAT, CURRENTLY, ARE NOT
National manager/Brand leader	
State manager	
Area leader	
Store manager	

Light bulbs

Actions

Chapter 8

Developing your team

As I hope has been highlighted earlier in this book, your ability to develop your team will be fundamental to your success.

It is essential to retain team members and build a career path for everyone in your team, so they each feel they have a bright future within the business. Without succession planning and career planning, you may be in danger of losing good people, especially if they have developed a need for growth. If your best people leave, you could be forced (out of desperation) to promote people into roles they are either not ready for or for which they lack the attributes needed to succeed. Alternatively, you might need to recruit externally to fill senior roles – which can be time-consuming and costly.

Identifying and developing future senior leaders

Many senior retail leaders have built incredible retail careers from starting out as casual team members. Many began with no aspirations or didn't consider that their future career would lie in the retail industry.

To have a reliable pool of future leaders, you need to look at people in the roles below the levels of seniority and responsibility for which you will eventually require a suitable leadership candidate. You need to identify the people who are suitable and begin to develop them so they will be ready to take on a leadership role.

From the leaders within your business, who have you identified as being likely successors for more senior roles? Depending on the size of your business, these could be the people who have the potential to fill the roles of area, state, national or general managers.

The diagram on the next page shows where the pool of potential talent needs to be found and the development needed for senior roles to be filled by people you identify as potential leaders.

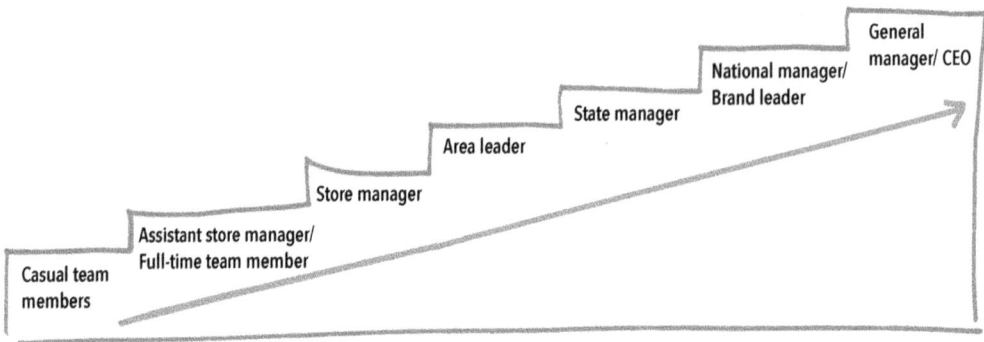

How can you ensure the right people are being identified as future leaders? What are you doing to mentor those people and provide them with the necessary opportunities to ensure they are ready for their next role? Are ongoing conversations being had to keep those people engaged and motivated to grow?

Online business network LinkedIn's senior director of talent development Stephanie Conway said of the 2023 data discussed in LinkedIn's report on *Global Talent Trends* that ' . . . employees consider career-development opportunities to be one of the top reasons to stay at – or leave – their company.'[10] Employees believe professional development to be the number-one way to improve company culture – so the consequences of neglecting development can be significant.

According to a 2019 report by the Execu|Search Group, 86% of professionals said that they would change jobs if a new company offered them more opportunities for professional development.[11]

10 Conway, S., October 2023, 'Trends in the labor market: Hiring around the world continues to decline', *Global Talent Trends* (Australia & New Zealand Edition): Data-driven insights into the changing world of work, LinkedIn, viewed 5 August 2024, <https://business.linkedin.com/en-au/talent-solutions/global-talent-trends>.

11 Execu|Search, 7 January 2019, "The Employee Experience will be Critical to Business Success in 2019, According to New Hiring Outlook Report by The Execu|Search Group", *PR Newswire*, viewed 5 August 2024, <https://www.prnewswire.com/news-releases/the-employee-experience-will-be-critical-to-business-success-in-2019-according-to-new-hiring-outlook-report-by-the-execusearch-group-300773946.html>.

Research carried out by Better Buys indicated that employees who are provided with professional development opportunities are 15% more engaged and have a 34% higher rate of retention than those who don't.[12]

Consider Deloitte's 2021 findings that:

> *Organizations with a strong learning culture are 92 percent more likely to develop novel products and processes, 52 percent more productive, 56 percent more likely to be the first to market with their products and services, and 17 percent more profitable than their peers. Their engagement and retention rates are also 30-50 percent higher.*[13]

As is raised in Chapter 9 ('Leading area leaders') and Chapter 6 ('Creating empowered leaders'), the right development and training can result in every one of the people you lead feeling empowered in their role. Leaders, in particular, have a high need for personal and professional growth and will leave if that need can't be met.

Later, in Chapter 11, 'The intergenerational workplace' (see page 167), it will be emphasised that opportunities for development, training, and growth in the workplace seem to be particularly important to Gen Z people (born about 1995–2012).

Evidently, prioritising learning and development is crucial to the business's bottom line – but providing learning and development doesn't need to be costly. You do, however, need to ensure that the professional development provided is personalised. In other words, make it relevant and ensure it is truly connected to each of your team members, rather than a mere box-ticking exercise.

As you saw in Chapter 5, 'Alignment with goals and plans', there are opportunities for on-the-job learning and growth in monthly planning meetings and I recommend that this learning and development, as well as a sense of ownership and belonging, be accelerated with quarterly two-day retreats (see pages 80–81).

12 BetterBuys, no date, "The impact of professional development", viewed 5 August 2024, <https://www.betterbuys.com/lms/professional-development-impact>.

13 Deloitte Insights, 25 January 2015, "Becoming irresistible: A new model for employee engagement", *Deloitte Review*, Issue 16, viewed 5 August 2024, <https://www2.deloitte.com/us/en/insights/deloitte-review/issue-16/employee-engagement-strategies.html>.

As was discussed in Chapter 4, 'People: The greatest business asset', growth (such as that involved in personal and career development) is considered to be one of the six human needs espoused by American career and business strategist Tony Robbins. Offering possibilities for growth and development will meet that need in your team members and leaders.

Career development

How often do you have career discussions with each of your leaders? How often are your leaders having career discussions with their team members? In many organisations, the topic of career development is often included as part of a yearly discussion and is linked to a performance review. I have heard of leaders giving performance feedback at the end of the year to people whose results have meant they will not be receiving their yearly bonus (refer to my comments on incentives in Chapter 10, 'Reward and recognition', for my thoughts on this). Giving feedback once annually doesn't enable people to improve their performance and only leaves them frustrated and disappointed.

Ideally, feedback on results and performance should be provided monthly – or at least quarterly, so that everyone can improve in their role and the opportunities for ongoing career discussions are provided.

University professor, researcher, public speaker and author Dr Brené Brown says in her book *Dare to lead. Brave work. Tough conversations. Whole hearts*,[14] giving feedback to the members of your team so they can improve is the kindest thing you can do for them.

Solving the leadership gaps in retail

For the retailers I work with, 50%–70% of their workforce is made up of casual team members. Having a large casual workforce does have its advantages. It provides flexibility and helps with managing costs – or so it seems!

Something that is crucial for the success of a retail business is having highly motivated store managers, but the most significant gaps occurring in the chain of leadership are caused by not having a solid succession plan for

---

14 Brown, Dr B., *Dare to lead. Brave work. Tough conversations. Whole hearts*, Random House, New York, NY, 2018.

filling store manager roles. You will probably have seen job advertisements on online business network sites saying something similar to 'Come and join our superstar team', or 'We are looking for passionate leaders to join our team'. Having seen many such advertisements it appears to me that, as retailers scramble to fill store manager roles (especially for regional stores), they all 'fish in the same pond' and are all trying to attract the same people externally because they are unable to fill those roles from within the business.

Although filling store manager roles is usually the responsibility of the area leader, if there is no succession plan in place to fill those roles when existing store managers move on or new stores are opened, the impact is eventually felt further up the chain of leadership. All leadership roles need to be filled with the right people and there needs to be a pool of great candidates to eventually fill roles at all levels of the leadership ladder.

Rethinking the mix of your store workforce

The greatest impact on the issue of filling store manager roles with the best candidates will be made by already having assistant manager roles filled with the right candidates to become store managers. Having an experienced team of assistant store managers provides the best opportunity for a retail business to fill store manager roles with the right people. With so much focus being on managing wage costs, it is usually the assistant store manager role that becomes redundant or is filled with a pseudo assistant store manager, who is often a casual team member taking on more responsibilities.

While managing wage costs is paramount in retail, I think there is a need to look at this strategy with fresh eyes. I want to highlight this because, when I speak to area leaders about this concept, it is obvious that a major barrier they face is the management of wage costs and the way that impacts their ability to have full-time assistant store managers in their stores so those people can gain the valuable experience necessary for them to be future store managers.

Not having in place a pool of assistant store managers who become capable enough in their roles to be ready to take on store manager roles contributes to the gaps in leadership that retail businesses experience.

One thing retailers could do is look at ways to recruit more full-time young people who are not studying. Those young people would then need to be motivated to stay and grow with the business, rather than the way those studying leave when they finish their studies to pursue their chosen careers. While this may be viewed as an additional cost, I often ask the question: 'Which cost is greater?'

- What price are you paying by not having high-performing store managers in every store?
- What lost opportunities could you attribute to having the wrong store managers in place?
- What are the long-term consequences of not having assistant store managers in stores?

Assistant store managers: One of the most crucial roles in retail

I maintain that not having a store manager, or having the wrong store manager, is a far greater cost to the business than the additional wage costs of having full-time assistant store managers.

Assistant store managers need to be considered as 'apprentice' store managers, meaning the role can't be filled by casuals acting as pseudo assistant store managers, who are working while studying full-time and who will leave the store to pursue their chosen career once they complete their studies.

Having people who want to pursue a retail career as the assistant store managers in stores is the way to best equip people to take on leadership roles and will ensure you have a great pool of potential store managers developing and growing with the business.

Rethinking the percentage of casual workers and relying on a larger percentage of full-time workers could avoid a lot of challenges down the track, especially when it comes to leadership.

FAQ: About Leadership

Q: Where do store managers come from?
A: Assistant store managers

Q: Where do area leaders come from?
A: Store managers

Q: Where do state managers come from?
A: Area leaders

Q: Where do national managers/general managers come from?
A: State managers

Lived lessons in leadership

I vividly remember a one-on-one conversation I had with Flight Centre's cofounder Geoff Harris very early in my career.

I had been performing well in my role and was hitting all of my targets. Geoff sat me down and asked me whether I had ever considered a role in leadership. He said that he felt I had great leadership potential, then started to articulate the qualities he saw in me.

'WOW!' I thought. 'Me a leader!'

I had never considered myself to be a leader. As I revealed in the 'Preface' to this book, I had always thought I was meant to be a teacher.

After the discussion with Geoff, I continued to work hard and within twelve months was promoted to the position of assistant store manager.

Twelve months after that, almost to the day, my manager relocated to Sydney. Geoff spoke to me again and indicated that he was very keen for me to take over the reins as manager of the store. He reminded me of the qualities he saw in me and really created in me the belief that I could be very successful in the store manager role. It was all very exciting – and frightening at the same time – to be given the responsibility of a team of eight travel consultants and a business that had a great amount of potential to grow and improve.

Being highly motivated to do a good job, I was completely driven by the new role and I worked even harder, trying to lead by example, developing a culture in which everyone in the team had ownership of the results, and creating an environment within which it was fun to work.

Had Geoff Harris never expressed the potential he saw in me during my early days in the business, I don't think I would have ever considered taking on a leadership role – and of course, I wanted to do the best job I could to repay him for the faith he had showed in me.

In my first full year as a store manager, the store's profits grew by 150%. At the end of the financial year, my team and I were up on stage at the company's end-of-financial-year ball, filled with pride to receive our plaque acknowledging our results.

Succession planning for senior leadership roles

One of the greatest stumbling blocks for senior leaders is not having potential leaders ready to fill leadership roles when needed, especially if the business is in a growth phase. Ask yourself:

- how much time you spend identifying and developing future leaders for senior roles
- how much time you spend having career conversations with the people you lead.

Recruiting externally for senior roles can be challenging, time-consuming and expensive. If leadership roles are not usually filled from within the business, it can send the wrong message about future career paths to your people and can damage your culture.

If you consider your team:

- do you know everyone in your team's career aspirations?
- do you have someone ready to step into every role in your team if roles become available?

If you are losing quality leaders to other organisations, that could indicate you do not have a solid succession plan in place and are not having career conversations with team members individually.

Again, I want to highlight that building a succession plan and filling leadership roles are the responsibility of operational leaders, not the human resources team.

Attributes senior leaders need to succeed

Before appointing anyone to a senior leadership role, consider whether they meet the criteria listed in the following checklist.

Put a tick in the column provided beside each description you think a potential leadership candidate fulfils.

SENIOR LEADERSHIP ATTRIBUTES	
DOES THE POTENTIAL LEADER:	
• **have serious motivation for doing the role?** Senior roles are not for the fainthearted. There should be no 'entitlement' involved (like next in line being promoted due to length of employment).	
• **have the ability to take responsibility for strategy?** Senior leaders need to understand that, the more senior the role, the more strategic ownership, accountability and responsibility there is.	
• **achieve very good results in their current role and display genuine growth as a leader from that experience?** Many senior leaders fail when they are in a hurry to get to the next role without spending enough time gaining experience and achieving results in their current role.	
• **cope when things are not going well and have a willingness to ask for guidance?** Having resilience and seeking support and advice is crucial in a competitive industry. Senior leaders need to be able to adapt quickly and bring their team with them.	
• **possess well-developed self-confidence/self-belief?** Leaders need to feel good about themselves and their ability to do the job. This doesn't mean they tick every box right now, but they do need to have self-confidence and a desire to learn and grow.	

(Continued on next page)

(Continued from previous page.)

DOES THE POTENTIAL LEADER:	
• **demonstrate strong self-discipline?** Self-discipline is crucial when setting expectations of others, leading by example, and establishing a consistent leadership style.	
• **understand the brand's customers, marketing, and brand strategy?** The positioning of the brand needs to be understood so strategies can be set and implemented confidently with the leadership team.	
• **have leadership ability?** There is no use trying to train and develop those that don't possess natural leadership ability (even if they are technically very good). It is important to identify the difference between technical skills and leadership skills. Those with great technical skills but no natural leadership skills will often struggle to lead others. This can be evident in those working in support roles, such as in finance or marketing for example.	
• **take responsibility for their own development?** A leader characteristically demonstrate a genuine desire to learn and grow and accepts ownership of developing their leadership skills.	

It is not a matter of every candidate fulfilling all the criteria from the outset. If you can see potential and ways in which a candidate can develop to fulfil more of what makes a good leader, use the checklist as a guide to ways in which you can assist that candidate to learn and develop.

Communication also plays a huge part in how your team members develop – and how they relate to you and engage with their role in the business (see Chapter 12, 'A system for communicating').

Light bulbs

Actions

Chapter 9

Leading area leaders

I have yet to speak to a senior retail leader who doesn't believe that the area leader role is the most influential in retail.

A statement similar to the following appeared in my first book, *The essential guide for area leaders in retail*:

> *Area leader roles are roles of influence rather than of control. Area leaders influence the behaviour of all the store managers and team members in their region. . . Fundamentally, area leaders are at the heart of a retailer's communication and are the source of all information relayed to stores from the support office. They communicate all areas of the organisation's support functions to stores and are the avenue for stores to provide feedback back to the providers of those various support functions.*

As a senior leader, regardless of whether area leaders report to you or not, you need to remember the importance of what your area leaders do for the business and the influence they have. Many of you will have been area leaders at some point in your career, so you will have experienced first-hand the challenges that area leaders experience. This chapter is intended to help you find ways to use what you know to set your area leaders up for success.

Part of your leadership role will involve setting the brand's strategy. It is crucial that the area leaders understand the strategy, take ownership of it, have a plan to implement it, and receive regular support and feedback. This is of major importance to the business.

Area leaders lead best when they have a plan that is aligned with the greater business plan and they are empowered to make decisions that they feel are best for their areas. They need to be able to set clear expectations of themselves and the stores within their areas and to manage those expectations. When area leaders feel empowered, rather than micromanaged, they perform at their best.

My experience has revealed four categories of area leaders based on the way they lead. So let's start by revisiting what I said about those four types of area leaders in my first book, *The essential guide for area leaders in retail*.

The four categories of area leaders

These pages are intended to help you recognise and understand characteristics of the different types of area leaders.

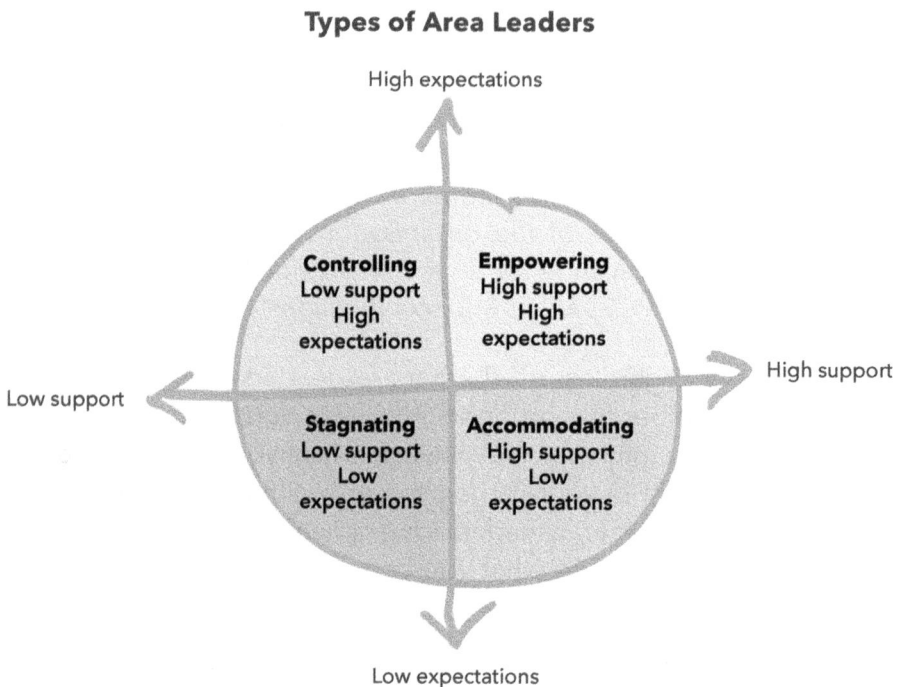

Types of Area Leaders

1 THE 'ACCOMMODATING' AREA LEADER
(HIGH SUPPORT AND LOW EXPECTATIONS)

An area leader categorised as 'accommodating' will be more focused on the environment of the stores in the region rather than on strategies.

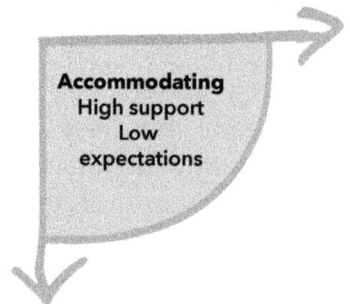

Leaders from this category want to do a great job and ensure the store teams feel well supported. However, to achieve this, these area leaders often create additional work for themselves and, as a result, work longer hours to get the job done.

These area leaders often have a need to be liked and to please the people with whom they deal. As a result, they often find it difficult to hold store managers accountable for shortfalls in meeting budget expectations, fearing that doing so would damage their relationship with them.

They want to feel as though they are supporting their stores and, as a result, will often take on too much responsibility – taking on tasks and roles that should be performed by the store managers. They become the 'fixer' for everything and find it difficult to deflect responsibility back to the store managers where it belongs.

Store visits are focused more on relationships with the store teams rather than on store results. These area leaders have a need for team harmony and they struggle to make difficult decisions for fear of being unpopular.

Many area leaders new to the role will display these types of attitudes and behaviours. If area leaders from this category stay in one place for too long, it may cause frustration – not only for the area leader but also for the store managers.

Typical symptoms of 'accommodating' area leaders might be:

- difficulty holding their stores accountable for shortfalls in results and standards
- struggling to have honest conversations with store leaders and team members
- inability to communicate clear expectations
- lack of adherence to brand standards by stores
- retention of underperforming team members and leaders.

The stores overseen by these area leaders are often nice places to work but they underperform in regard to budget projections, with low standards often being accepted.

Store managers who are high achievers will often feel frustrated by how little their area leader expects of them and the lack of the setting of higher targets for which to aim.

2 THE 'CONTROLLING' AREA LEADER (LOW SUPPORT AND HIGH EXPECTATIONS)

An area leader categorised as 'controlling' will be focused on results rather than store environments.

Controlling
Low support
High
expectations

Leaders from this category will probably feel discouraged when stores in their region are not achieving their budget projections.

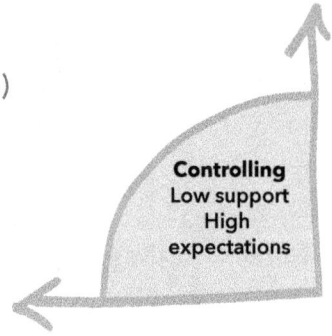

Often, this type of area leader was once a very good store manager, leading to frustration when the store managers they oversee are not doing the job as well as they did. As a result, 'controlling' area leaders tend to put additional pressure on store managers, who then become fearful, demotivated and feel as if their voices are being disregarded and their opinions ignored. Store managers experiencing this feel that they don't have the support they need to achieve what is expected of them. This can create a 'them and us' mentality between store managers and their area leaders. When the pressure increases, it is likely that some store managers will want to step down from their positions or may leave the business altogether, leaving the area leader with the task of finding suitable replacements.

Typical symptoms of 'controlling' area leaders might be:

- focusing on KPIs and results, but not providing stores with clear strategies for achieving them
- store managers being unclear as to what degree of autonomy they have and which decisions they are able to make independently
- accepting store managers doing only what is required of them without going above and beyond for the customer or the organisation
- an evident lack of teamwork and harmony in the stores in their regions
- a constant need to put out spot fires at store level that result from some of the symptoms listed above.

3 THE 'STAGNATING' AREA LEADER (LOW SUPPORT AND LOW EXPECTATIONS)

Stagnating
Low support
Low expectations

An area leader categorised as 'stagnating' will appear inconsistent in regard to the environments and strategies of their region.

Leaders from this category probably have no systems or strategies in place.

They may have been in the role for some time and have already tried the different styles described in the other three quadrants of the diagram, but with no success.

These types of area leaders have lost sight of the purpose of their role and are unclear regarding the outcomes they want to achieve. They will, at times, feel overwhelmed – so overwhelmed that they find it difficult to stay focused on a task and will be constantly trying to 'tick boxes' as an indicator of achievement, while feeling confused as to why they aren't actually achieving anything. They may develop a fixed mindset that there is a lack of reward for effort in their role.

If they can't find ways to make their roles work for them, these people will likely step down from their area leader positions or leave the organisation.

Typical symptoms of 'stagnating' area leaders might be:

- low team member engagement and little desire to achieve budgets
- high turnover, particularly among store managers
- disharmony or frustration among team members
- disengagement with the area leader role and its purpose.

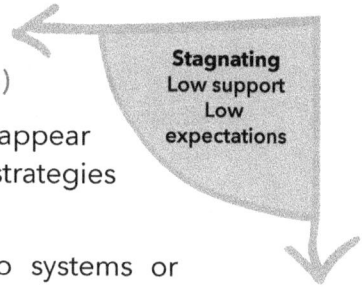

4 THE 'EMPOWERING' AREA LEADER (HIGH SUPPORT AND HIGH EXPECTATIONS)

Empowering
High support
High expectations

An area leader categorised as 'empowering' will be responsible for balance between the creation of a great working environment and implementation of strategies that achieve results.

Typically, those leading from this category deliver the best results. They are able to create and maintain high performing stores, regardless of their customer demographic or location. They take complete ownership of their region and its results.

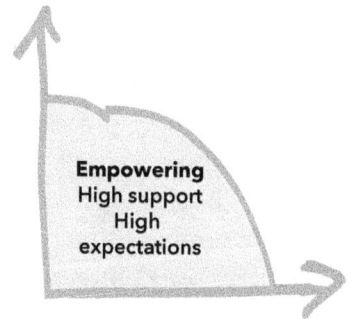

These area leaders develop store managers who take full responsibility for results, deliver a consistent customer experience and create an environment that makes their stores great places to work. They demonstrate a genuine care for the organisation's brand.

Ultimately, these area leaders are able to achieve results by providing high levels of support in order to achieve the high expectations they have of their store managers and teams.

'Empowering' area leaders will:

- be highly driven to achieve
- deliver or exceed their budget expectations
- take ownership of and responsibility for their region and will believe in the company's goals and vision
- be passionate about the company brand and will find purpose in the area leader role
- be highly respected by their people and their peers.

The development of area leaders

As an extension to the four categories of leaders referred to in the diagram on page 130, and discussed on the previous pages, the traits that will now be discussed (some of which overlap those already discussed) are what I typically see once area leaders have been appointed to that role.

The diagram on the next page provides common descriptions of area leaders at different stages of their development, along with the corresponding focus at each level and the effect leaders of that kind have on the desired results. All new area leaders begin at the 'Learning' stage and some progress 'upstream' while others are washed downstream. The 'Damaging' area leaders can cost the business money but, as area leaders progress towards becoming 'Empowering' area leaders, their effect on the business becomes more positive (and more profitable). The ideal is for area leaders to progress upward along this development path ('swim upstream'), but there are some who do slide backwards ('get washed downstream') as a result of lack of support, burnout or complacency (among other things).

The development of area leaders

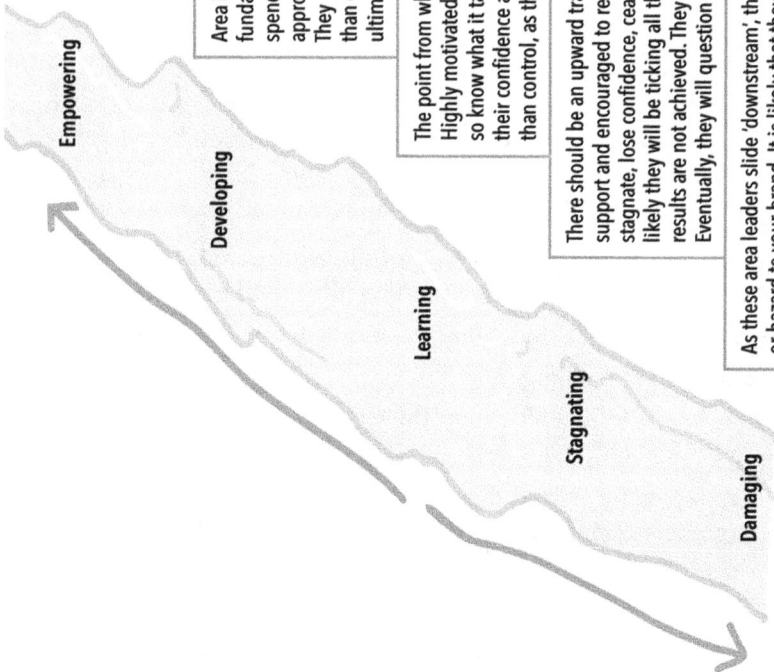

Stage	Description	FOCUS	EFFECT ON BUDGET RESULTS
Empowering	Area leaders at this level usually have a strong appetite for growth so, after they have implemented a systemised and focused approach to their role and are achieving great results, there will be a risk of losing them if their need for growth cannot be met.	Expectations	$$$
Developing	Area leaders grow and develop at this level, understanding the role's fundamentals. They begin to appreciate the need to adapt how they spend their time. They must focus on how to implement a systemised approach to their role and build structures to achieve consistency. They come to understand their role is now a role of influence rather than of control. How they prioritise and plan their store visits will ultimately determine their success.	Systems	$$
Learning	The point from which most area leaders commence their area leader journey. Highly motivated to do a great job, they may have been successful store managers so know what it takes to lead a great store. Development at this stage will grow their confidence and assist them to develop skills in leading with influence rather than control, as they grow to lead a region of stores – not just one.	Confidence	0
Stagnating	There should be an upward trajectory for a successful area leader but, if they are not given support and encouraged to retain 'Learning' status, they will be washed 'downstream, stagnate, lose confidence, cease to develop and feel unsure of themselves in the role. It is likely they will be ticking all the boxes and working hard, but will become frustrated when results are not achieved. They spend their time putting out spot fires and working long hours. Eventually, they will question whether the role is right for them.	Decision	–$
Damaging	As these area leaders slide 'downstream', their mindset becomes more negative. They can become a liability or hazard to your brand. It is likely that they will eventually need to be replaced before their negativity spreads throughout the area they lead.	Replace	–$$

Investing in area leader development

More investment needs to be made in this crucial group of retail leaders to prevent them from burning out, stagnating, and ultimately leaving the role or the business altogether.

Very little of the training budget is spent on area leaders – and the assumption is often made that a great store manager will naturally transition into a great area leader. What needs to be acknowledged is that a different skillset is required for a leader to successfully transition from leading one team to leading many.

Without blowing my own trumpet, retailers have seen a significant improvement in their area leaders' results after those leaders have completed my Ultimate Area Leader program. The retailers have noticed higher engagement, more confidence, improved structure and discipline among the teams, and that the area leaders are far less stressed due to having learned a structured way of fulfilling the role. Most notably, the number of calls from area leaders to the human resources team for assistance with solving people problems has significantly reduced.

Case Study: **Sue**

I recently worked with a national retailer who, due to the amount of people issues being experienced, had engaged me to work with the area leader team. Like many retailers, this business was experiencing a high turnover of people, especially store managers, and many issues with people were being escalated to be handled by the human resources team.

Sue was that retailer's head of people and culture and was particularly concerned with the increasing number of phone calls about issues relating to people that she was receiving from area leaders.

I was engaged to facilitate my four-day Ultimate Area Leader program, which is delivered over three months and is aimed at teaching people to become empowering area leaders (see pages 133–4).

The first day and a half of the program is focused on building the business environment (see pages 28–31).

After the area leaders had completed the first two days of the four-day Ultimate Area Leader program, Sue noticed an immediate reduction in the calls she was receiving from area leaders needing help and advice.

I asked what she thought had made the difference and she shared with me that she believed area leaders were seeing their store visits differently. They were using store visits to connect with their teams, especially their casual and part-time team members, and were also having meaningful conversations with store managers and starting to empower them to run their own stores.

It was obvious to me that the completion of the first two days of the program had already created a shift in the perception of the importance of building an environment. The retailer's area leaders had already begun to make changes to create environments in which people felt valued and had a sense of belonging to their team and brand.

When area leaders have greater exposure to the whole of the business, they gain an increased understanding of how and why decisions are made.

Through trial and error, some new area leaders will be able to figure out for themselves how to successfully transition from store manager to area leader to meet the expectations of the role. However, this usually requires working long hours, which is unsustainable and leads to a perceived lack of reward for effort – and burnout! To fast-track development, targeted training specific to the area leader role can be highly beneficial.

Reasons why area leaders don't succeed

I have always believed the role of area leader is the best job in the world when done well. Over recent years, I have trained over 700 area leaders across retail brands of all shapes and sizes. Undoubtedly, there is a very clear difference between those leaders who succeed and those who don't.

From my experience, there are some common traits, behaviours and approaches that definitely contribute to the failure of area leaders and, often, to their eventual departure from the role or from the organisation altogether. Some of these appear in the following list.

1   Not identifying, preparing or developing the skills needed to transition from store manager to area leader successfully.

2   They were not involved in creating the brand strategy and didn't understand the 'why' behind what they would ultimately be responsible for implementing in their stores.

3   Experiencing more pressure to achieve results with reduced resources.

4   Limited wage budgets, often resulting in the need for them to step in to fulfil responsibilities that the store manager and the in-store team should fulfil.

5   Feeling undervalued and not appreciated or acknowledged, especially when they *are* delivering very good results.

6   Not feeling empowered to make decisions that are best for their stores. Needing to defer approval for basic operational decisions to their leader.

7   Not being involved in the budget process for their region but being accountable for delivery of the budgeted results.

8   Feeling micromanaged and spending significant time on administrative tasks that do not add value to their results.

9   Being expected to be in stores constantly, without allowing time to plan and prepare for store visits and working on their business, requiring them to work long hours.

10 Not being rewarded adequately when they *are* achieving great results.

From experience, I have noted the following characteristics that distinguish successful area leaders from those who are not successful.

DIFFERENCES BETWEEN SUCCESSFUL AND UNSUCCESFUL AREA LEADERS	
AREA LEADERS WHO SUCCEED:	**AREA LEADERS WHO FAIL:**
• understand the role and are given support and regular feedback on their own performance	• are running multiple stores the same way they led one store, so are acting like expensive store managers
• feel 'invested in' as a result of regular training and feedback	• are often working solo, without receiving feedback, and feel isolated
• have a high need for growth and aspire to grow with the business	• have lost sight of why they wanted to become an area leader

AREA LEADERS WHO SUCCEED:	AREA LEADERS WHO FAIL:
• are empowered to make decisions relative to their role	• feel micromanaged and are unclear of what decisions they can make
• are clear about what is expected of them in their role	• have clarity regarding what is expected of them, but don't believe those expectations are realistic
• are involved in the brand strategy so they can understand why decisions are made	• don't understand why decisions that they are required to implement are being made
• have innate confidence in their own ability	• lack confidence and feel unsure of themselves
• can set expectations and aim to be respected by those they lead	• have a high need to be liked which impacts the ability to hold people accountable
• have a growth mindset and can quickly adapt to change	• have a fixed mindset and blame external factors for poor results
• have the ability to influence those they lead	• feel the need to be in control of those they lead
• understand the importance of human connection and building community	• don't value human connection and focus solely on KPIs
• have a disciplined approach to how they spend their time	• don't spend time planning ahead and preparing, operating only from day-to-day
• are able to maintain a consistent and structured approach to their store visits	• are inconsistent in how they schedule and structure their store visits
• know the KPIs and results for their area as a whole, not just store by store	• only focus on the KPIs and results day by day and are then reactive when results are not achieved
• actively work on succession plans for filling future store manager and assistant store manager roles	• are reactive when filling store manager and assistant store manager roles, meaning they are often forced to promote people who are not ready
• understand the important role played by casual team members and focus on building relationships with them	• see their casual team members as just a means to an end

How to help area leaders succeed

It makes good business sense to invest time and training in your area leaders and ensure they demonstrate positive behaviours that will deliver results.

My first book, *The essential guide for area leaders in retail*, is filled with strategies aimed at helping area leaders succeed. It was designed to be a prescriptive 'how to' guide aimed specifically at assisting area leaders, so I won't refer to what area leaders should and shouldn't be doing again here. However, I do need to say that I have been thrilled with the feedback I have received from area leaders for whom reading the book has positively impacted the way they lead, how they organise their time and their creation of a systemised approach to their role.

In this book, I would like the focus to be on sharing strategies that will help leaders of area leaders to do better in helping their area leaders succeed.

Retailers need to continually find ways to manage costs, and one of the biggest opportunities to manage costs is for individual area leaders to develop the capacity to lead larger areas. An area leader might currently be leading eight stores but could learn a systemised approach to the role that would give them the ability to increase the number of stores they lead. I also believe that if area leaders can lead larger areas, this will help prevent them from micromanaging their stores, allowing store managers to take more responsibility and preventing the area leaders from acting like very expensive casual store managers.

Many area leaders I have trained to become empowering area leaders, leading with a systemised approach to their role, now lead much bigger areas than they once did, are achieving great results and are saving the business significant amounts of money.

On the other hand, there have been area leaders I have trained in this approach who, once they returned to their role, were not given permission to implement what they had learned, which left them feeling frustrated and micromanaged.

My aim is to prevent area leaders from going in the 'downstream' direction and eventually stagnating and becoming a liability to your brand, as described by the 'Development of area leaders' diagram on page 135.

The goal is to help retailers by providing the right development, training and support to empower all leaders to deliver strong, consistent results.

The following tips are designed to expand your thinking, give rise to some interesting conversations, and suggest opportunities for improving the environment you provide for area leaders. Whether you feel it appropriate to implement these strategies will depend on where your area leaders are currently positioned on the 'Development of area leaders' scale, as described by the diagram already referred to, and whether you foresee the suggested strategies will help them to become 'empowered'.

1   **Invest in developing area leaders:** Your best store managers are often promoted to the area leader role. Don't assume that a successful store manager will be able to successfully make the transition to the role of area leader.

    It is crucial to acknowledge that the skills required to succeed in the area leader role are quite different from those of a successful store manager. Area leaders also have a high need for personal and professional growth and will leave if that need isn't met.

2   **Consider how empowered your area managers are:** There is a disconnect between how empowered *you* think area leaders are and how empowered *they* believe themselves to be.

    Do area leaders have clarity about the kinds of decisions they feel they can and cannot make?

    Do you receive many calls from area leaders asking questions you would assume they should be able to answer for themselves? Do they defer making decisions for fear of 'getting it wrong'? This is worth reflecting on and following up, because it could indicate the level of empowerment they have or perceive themselves to have.

3   **Encourage autonomy, rather than micromanaging:** Based on where your area leaders are positioned, compared to the levels described by the 'Development of area leaders' diagram discussed above (appearing on page 135), what decisions would you be comfortable with area leaders making that they are currently unable to make?

    Do your area leaders have an appropriate level of autonomy for the results you are asking them to deliver?

4 **Set clear expectations, create ownership and build accountability.**
Ensure area leaders understand what is expected of them.

To achieve success, everyone needs defined roles, with clear
expectations in regard to KPIs. The more levels of leadership
there are in your business, the more potential there will be for
micromanaging or overly complicated decision-making.

The ability to hold area leaders accountable is usually directly
proportional to their level of 'buy-in' for the business strategy
and the area's goals. For example, it's harder to hold someone
accountable for budget targets for which they don't feel ownership
or into which they have had no input.

5 **Encourage buy-in to results:** Working with their state and national
managers, area leaders should be involved in the budgeting process
for their area (annually, quarterly, and monthly). Their involvement
may be gradual, but it is crucial for growing their business acumen.
This is one of the most fundamental opportunities to positively
impact the area leader experience and its effect on results.

6 **Provide brand-based state and/or national recognition:** Deliver
monthly area leader recognition, linked to results across brands/
businesses, which acknowledges the monthly results for the area
and is communicated across the brand. For example, acknowledge
area leaders with the most growth in sales, or with the greatest
number of stores hitting or exceeding budget, etc. Focus on
whatever KPIs you decide should be a focus for recognition (refer
to the alignment with goals, discussed in Chapter 5, 'Alignment with
goals and plans').

7 **Allow area leaders time to work on the business (WOB):** During
my Ultimate Area Leader training program, I introduce and discuss
what is referred to by the acronym 'WOB' – 'work on business'. Allow
area leaders time at the start of each month to dedicate to working
on their business – reviewing the month that's been and planning
for the month ahead. This will give them a clear picture of how each
of their stores is tracking and what needs attention. This WOB time
can be one of the biggest game changers for area leaders and
influences how positively motivated and focused they are for the
month ahead.

8   **Schedule monthly one-on-ones with area leaders:** To help with
their development, area leaders should participate in a structured
monthly one-on-one with their leader. The discussion could be just a
regular check-in, but it also needs to focus on their area strategy and
determine whether they are on track to meet budgets or provide
strategies to assist if they aren't. Giving regular feedback on their
performance will help area leaders grow in their role. Having regular
one-on-one time with their leader also creates a sense of enormous
significance for them and for the importance of their role.

9   **Monthly area-based store manager meetings:** Many of the
challenges area leaders face could be addressed if they were
given the autonomy and budget to hold monthly area-based
meetings with their store managers (ideally face-to-face). Refer to
Chapter 12, 'A system for communicating', for more details about
these meetings.

Store manager meetings are potentially one of the biggest game
changers for area leaders (and their results), They should not be
seen as representing an unnecessary cost to the business but as the
greatest investment that can be made in ticking off all of Robbins'
'six core human needs' (discussed in Chapter 4, 'People: The
greatest business asset'; see pages 54–6).

10   **Allow area leaders to invest in their casual workforce:** Casuals can
be the most valuable people to any retailer, because they often
make up as much as 70% of its workforce. Find ways to enable your
area leaders to invest more time and money in this important group
of team members. Area leaders need your support in ensuring your
casual team members feel a real part of the store and the area; and
emotionally connect to the business's brand and its success.

11   **Incentive-based salaries:** Many area leaders leave the role due
to a perceived lack of reward for effort. I want to reinforce the
importance of having incentives linked to growth in results. Refer to
Chapter 10 'Reward and recognition', for more information on the
DOs and DON'Ts of incentive-based payments (see pages 155–6).

12   **Elevate the area leader role:** Area leaders need to understand the
important work they do and the influence their role has. They need
to have the mindset that they are senior business leaders.

Lived lessons in leadership

I trained the Queensland state manager and the area leaders of a national retail brand using my Ultimate Area Leader program – a four-day program delivered over three months (one day a month).

Day three of the program is primarily dedicated to planning, prioritising and delivering impactful store visits and that is when I introduce the concept of 'WOB' or 'working on business' (refer to page 63 of my book *The essential guide for area leaders in retail*). The concept of WOB and prioritising their time is a crucial part of setting area leaders up for success over the month following their WOB day.

It was approximately six months later, when I was back in the support office of the same retailer working with another of their brands, that I noticed a group of area leaders I had worked with previously all gathered in a meeting room. I popped my head in the door and they excitedly shared with me that they were all doing their WOB, reflecting on the month that had been and preparing for the month ahead.

They told me how just scheduling that time per month had transformed the way they worked. Each of those area leaders shared with me how they felt more organised and had a better handle on what was happening in each of their stores, meaning they were able to prioritise which stores they needed to visit and exactly what they needed to focus on. It also created more discussion and collaboration at the end of each month to help problem solve and find shared learnings.

Since taking time monthly to WOB, they were more focused and energised – and felt less overwhelmed and stressed.

Leading area leaders checklist

On the next page is a checklist to help ensure that your area leaders are set up for success. This checklist is designed to help you consider how you can better support area leaders in their roles, build their confidence, develop their skills, and empower them to lead more effectively.

Put a tick in the column provided beside each of the descriptions you think applies to you as a leader of area leaders.

The descriptions in the checklist are designed to help you identify opportunities for developing your approach to leading area leaders. There is space for you to add any other aspects of your leadership role that you think need to be included.

LEADING AREA LEADERS CHECKLIST	
I invest time and budget into specific development of the area leader role.	
I have scheduled, planned monthly one-on-ones with each area leader who reports to me.	
My store visits are primarily for the purpose of spending time developing the area leader.	
Area leaders are involved in the budgeting process for their areas.	
Area leaders receive meaningful recognition for their results.	
Area leaders are clear on what is expected of them in their roles.	
Area leaders are clear about which decisions they can make for their area.	
Area leaders are empowered to make appropriate decisions that impact their area.	
Area leaders are empowered to take time to work on their business (WOB) each month.	
Area leaders have budgeted money to spend on their casual workforce to improve engagement and retention.	
Area leaders are adequately incentivised and financially rewarded for attaining their results.	
Area leaders have succession plans identifying future store managers and assistant store managers.	
Area leaders create development opportunities for future store managers.	
Area leaders understand their area's annual budget, week by week, month by month, or store by store; rather than just day by day.	
I have identified potential future area leaders and I invest time in their development and career planning for future roles.	

Light bulbs

Actions

Chapter 10
Reward and recognition

I spent twenty-five years working for a retailer for whom reward and recognition were at the core of the culture.

I am convinced, that it was recognition and acknowledgement that drove the business's success as much as financial incentives did. When reward and recognition work together the combination can create outstanding results.

REWARD

A reward is an external motivator – in other words, 'If you do this, then *you will get that*.' Incentives and incentive-based salaries are a means of ensuring people are rewarded for their results. However, it is important to recognise that incentives alone do not work to keep people motivated long-term. I have seen incentives used poorly to change behaviour or drive results but, if incentives alone are used, as soon as the incentive is no longer offered people usually revert to their previous behaviour. Individual incentives can work well to achieve results in the short-term but, when they are also associated with team incentives, better outcomes are usually achieved.

RECOGNITION

Recognition is about acknowledgment of work done and contributions made to results. While reward is an external motivator, recognition is an intrinsic one, meeting people's need for significance – making people *feel valued* for their contribution. My experience is that most people will work harder to achieve recognition than they do for a reward. The effort individuals and teams will put into receiving an inexpensive trophy or award is often incredible (particularly in the cases of team-oriented awards).

There are many ways to both recognise and reward your people. This chapter will touch on some of them.

Using reward and recognition to create healthy competition

Lived lessons in leadership

I joined Flight Centre as a novice travel consultant. For the first three months, my wage was $150 per week and 40% commission on whatever travel I sold. It was obvious by the pay structure that making sales was a big part of the culture and the ability to sell was crucial to personal and team success.

Not all new consultants survived the first three months in the job, but the earnings of those who did changed after that first three months to be 50% salary and 50% commission. Like many, not only did I survive but I thrived. I loved that I had significant control over my income and that my effort and results were rewarded with what I earned. Although I was part of a store team, I felt like I was running my own little business within a business.

Before joining Flight Centre, I was certain that I wanted to be teacher. The Flight Centre job was a far cry from the school/teaching culture I had left behind, in which the fixed salary didn't change no matter how hard you worked, the amount of effort you put in or the results that were obtained by your students. Teachers were paid based on longevity in the role rather than on their results. But reward and recognition were huge in the Flight Centre culture, driving attainment of both sales and commission.

My experience as a young consultant at Flight Centre was my first exposure to feeling completely empowered. That was a win/win situation because, the more I earned for myself, the more profitable my team was and the more money the business made.

All the store teams in the area would come together on the first Wednesday of each month, on what were known as 'buzz nights'. We would gather at a city restaurant and enjoy a bowl of pasta together. Those nights were sponsored by different suppliers who would present updates on their product to us but, most importantly, company cofounder Geoff Harris would announce and acknowledge the top performers for the month. Those lists included the top sales results; the most profitable stores, the most improved stores, and 'personal best' sales results (an award highlighting that we were competing with our own past results as well as the results of others). It was always a great thrill to have your name read out – and positive team feeling was created by celebrating the achievements of others.

I am convinced that this kind of recognition was as big a driver of results as the financial rewards that came with it. Being financially rewarded for your results, as well as being recognised for them, was the cornerstone of Flight Centre's success.

As described in 'Lived lessons in leadership' on the facing page, 'buzz nights' were area gatherings held at the start of every month, for which area leaders were responsible for running in their own areas. Team members across the region came together at a local venue, such as a pub or restaurant.

A supplier would be invited to attend and sponsor the night to provide an update on their product. There was always a waitlist for suppliers to sponsor Flight Centre's buzz nights because it was both cost-effective and time-effective for them to address a large group of salespeople in one place, at one time. The suppliers who took advantage of the opportunity saw an immediate spike in sales following a buzz night.

But, the real purpose of the buzz nights was to recognise the best results achieved by individuals and teams for the preceding month. As was described in 'Lived lessons in leadership' on the facing page, recognition was given to the most profitable stores and the most improved stores, but the highest sales of a particular product was also included if it aligned with a strategy that was a focus that month. Individual awards included high sales, most improved sales, and top novice performers.

Team members would focus on increasing their sales throughout the month so they could be acknowledged at a buzz night. Each person or team would be recognised in front of their peers and team members loved all being recognised together as part of a team.

All the monthly award results were accumulated and the top performers for the whole year would be recognised as the 'best of the best' at Flight Centre's end-of-financial-year ball.

In my last year as national leader of 'Vicmania' (see pages 12–13), I had eleven area leaders each holding a monthly buzz night. My total budget for buzz nights for the financial year across 'Vicmania' was $230,000. That budget being such a significant amount of money illustrates how much buzz nights were valued – and every cent that was invested in those nights was worth it, because they were key drivers of sales and profit.

The buzz nights also assisted with meeting Tony Robbins' 'six core human needs' for team members, as explained in Chapter 4 – particularly the needs for 'significance', 'connection' and 'contribution'.

Incentives and recognition

90% of something is better than 100% of nothing

When I was promoted to my first store manager role at Flight Centre, I received a team leader wage, a commission for my sales and a 10% profit share of the store profit results. The more profit my team made, the more I earned.

This was incredibly empowering because it took the ownership of my role to another level. I felt like a true business owner – spiritually anyway!

All KPIs, such as sales and commission, margins, expenses, and profit, were transparent and shared with all teams. Not only did I have complete access to and understanding of my own store's results, but I also had the same access and understanding for the results of other stores. That made for healthy competition between stores.

As part of building their financial acumen, each store manager was involved in the budgeting process before the commencement of each new financial year. Individual store managers would sit with their area leader and accountant to work on the store budget for the following year. The goal, of course, was to improve on the results of the previous year and to look for opportunities to grow sales and reduce expenses. Each quarter's performance would be reviewed to ensure results were on track. What the KPIs were saying helped decide the individual strategy each store manager needed to implement in the next financial year.

Store managers were given ownership of the results through their involvement with the budgeting process and, as a result, were also held accountable for the good, the bad, and the ugly of the results. So as a store manager, having ownership of the store budget, I was also held accountable for delivering the results dependent on it. I needed to ensure that my in-store team members didn't waste money and kept our expenses to a minimum, because that also affected store profits. Not only did I need to understand this but I also needed my team to understand it.

If I felt empowered, there was no reason why my team couldn't feel empowered too.

As part of our strategy to grow our results, the whole store team would meet weekly at a time before the store opened. We would look at our results and plan strategies for the week ahead so we could keep track of how we were performing. As a team, we would decide on actions and strategies to ensure we hit our KPI goals. Some strategies were about growing sales, and some were about eliminating waste.

At the end of the month, once the results were finalised, I would share them with my team. I would give each team member a copy of the expenses, and, together, we would analyse where we could save money.

I was amazed at some of the crazy things my team did to save money! For example, the team was blown away by how much our phone bill was each month (remember, this was at a time when a business paid for each call made). My team came up with some great strategies to reduce the phone bill and, within a couple of months, our phone bill was reduced by a third. Many other great initiatives were developed from this strategy of analysing finances as a team.

We would look at what products we were selling well and those that we weren't converting to sales. We would then put some specific training in place to address the conversion problems, often inviting 'experts' to share their knowledge on particular products.

I'm not advocating that all retailers give away 10% of their profits to store managers (which was the incentive I received as a store manager), or implement exactly any of the approaches I have shared, but it is worth considering the way you currently financially incentivise your leaders and how you could reward their good results in a more meaningful way.

It is worth considering:

- how healthy competition can be encouraged between stores and the achievement of good results can be recognised
- how an environment can be created in which store managers take more ownership, accountability and responsibility for their results
- how recognition of achievements can be used more effectively to drive sales and profit
- how store managers can regularly share information about results with their teams to increase team engagement.

Incentives and retention

Many retailers offer incentives as part of their salary packages.

Incentive-based salaries should be a very effective way of ensuring everyone is in control of their own earnings. Because income is a direct result of personal performance, everyone aims to perform well. Those who achieve good performances will earn good incomes; and those who perform exceptionally well will earn exceptional incomes. The reverse is also true – those who are not performing as well will earn less. Unless leaders can improve their performance, they are likely to leave to find more certainty in roles for which their income will be guaranteed irrespective of how well they do the job.

Incentive-based wage systems don't totally solve performance issues, but they certainly allow individuals to take responsibility for their earnings. If you have a very good incentive-based salary system in place you should never lose a good performer to a competitor because of the offer of more money. Everyone should be in control of their own earnings.

Most retail leaders do have an incentive component to their salary package; however, in many cases, the incentive part of the salary is very small, so there isn't a huge difference in salary between average performance and high performance. There is an enormous opportunity for retailers to consider ways they can financially reward their leaders so there is more upside for those leaders financially.

THE EXTRA EFFORT PEOPLE WILL PUT IN FOR A $20 PLAQUE

I quickly understood the power of recognition when, at the end of each financial year, stores and areas would receive recognition in a very public way at Flight Centre's end-of-financial-year ball. Award categories were set at the start of each financial year. These would include most profitable stores, most improved stores, new store performance awards, outstanding team awards and individual achievement awards. Acknowledgement for individual performances included awards for people who had achieved the highest sales and the most improved results.

Each award was a plaque acknowledging the individual or team for their achievement. Most importantly, people were presented with their plaques on stage in front of their peers.

The monthly 'buzz nights' (see page 151) had provided a monthly focus for ongoing recognition that culminated with these annual awards recognising the performances over the whole financial year. The awards were a significant motivator and driver of results. Incentives of this kind, recognising contributions to the business, not only motivate people to attain and surpass expected results but they also help the business to retain the best people.

Over twenty-five years of being part of that Flight Centre culture of reward and recognition, I learned that there was a difference between the two but that each played an equally important role in keeping people motivated and driving results.

When reward and recognition work together, magic happens, and sustained results can be achieved long-term. This can have an enormous positive impact on your culture.

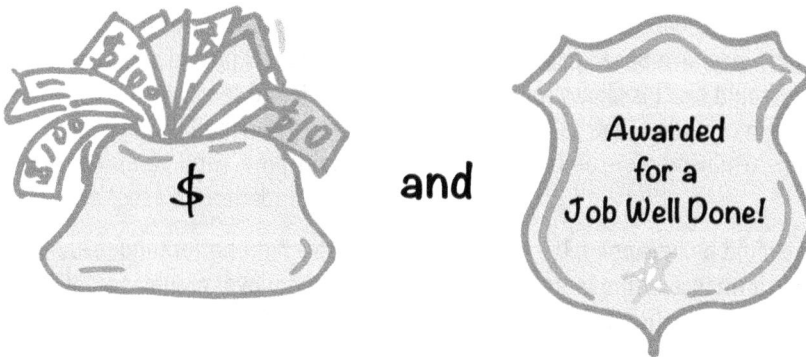

The DOs and DON'Ts of reward and recognition

I can't recommend anything specific that will ensure you retain your best leaders or improve your results, because every retailer is different – be it in size, goals, longevity, or any number of other factors. The culture of some retailers may be aligned with incentive-based salaries for leaders and team members, while the culture of other retailers may not be.

I have learned from experience some of the benefits and pitfalls of incentive-based salaries. The following are some lessons I have learned about 'what to do' and 'what not to do' when it comes to incentives for various leaders, including store managers, area leaders and senior leaders. How this advice is applied must be considered relative to each of those roles and with consideration of your business structure and culture.

INCENTIVES	
THE DOS	**THE DON'TS**
Incentives must be linked to measurable results or KPIs.	Incentives should not be fluffy or subjective. They need to be measurable and worth aspiring to.
Incentives should be paid monthly and can be adjusted quarterly. This keeps leaders motivated and helps them maintain focus.	Avoid only paying incentive bonuses quarterly or annually, because long-term incentives will not keep people motivated and won't maintain their focus for a sustained period of time.
The more senior the leader, the more significant the incentive-based portion of their salary should be. This allows senior leaders to be in control of their salary and work towards achieving more ambitious goals.	Avoid payment structures based on high retainers and low incentives because these do not challenge senior leaders to perform, nor do they allow them to have more control over their income. High performers could be lured to a competitor for a higher salary.
Incentives should be uncapped. The better a leader's performance is, the more they should be able to earn. (Remember 90% of something is better than 100% of nothing.)	Never lose a high-performing leader to a competitor over money. Incentives should not be capped as long as they are proportionally aligned with the delivery of financial results.
If incentives are linked to KPIs, such as sales and/or profit, they must also be linked to the budgeting process and the outcomes the business is aimed at achieving. The budget must feel achievable, while still representing a stretch that requires effort to achieve.	Finance and human resources teams can be a great sounding board when designing incentives, especially incentives for store managers and area leaders, but the design of incentives and the implementation of them must be the responsibility of the operations team.
Incentives must be simple to understand and linked to the KPIs on which the business is focused.	Never overcomplicate incentives with measuring too many KPIs. That becomes confusing and reduces the impact of the incentives.

Area leader reward and recognition

As I have said a number of times previously, the area leader role is the most influential in retail. Yet many retailers do not adequately reward or recognise the contribution made by these influential leaders.

Several retailers acknowledge the high turnover of their area leaders as being one of their greatest challenges; and see increasing area leader retention as being an opportunity to improve results.

I have conducted significant research into what would make the biggest difference to area leader engagement. My research suggests that area leaders need to be:

1   adequately rewarded for their results

2   adequately recognised for their results, in a meaningful way.

Whatever 'adequately' is interpreted to mean depends on the circumstances of the business, the business's senior leaders and the individual area leaders involved.

To assist with defining 'adequate', the following text deals with situations in which reward and recognition are 'inadequate'.

Failure to reward results

A failure to reward results occurs when the money they 'earn' does not adequately reward someone for their job and the results they have achieved. This means there is not enough upside to the person's salary, even though they are achieving great results. As a result of the lack of incentives and the inability to earn a greater income despite doing a very good job, these insufficiently rewarded leaders look to move to a competitor's business where they will receive more money, or to a role involving less pressure.

As I have already highlighted, money alone will not keep area leaders in their roles if other needs are not being met. But monetary reward in the form of incentive payments and increased monetary rewards if they are performing well is still a great way to give area leaders ownership and control of their incomes. It will also assist you in retaining your best area leaders and attracting external candidates who have a high need for growth and believe in their own abilities.

Failure to recognise results

Aside from insufficient monetary rewards, many leaders feel they also lack appropriate recognition. Many feel that, despite their achievements, they are not receiving adequate acknowledgment for results.

Depending on the size of the business, implementation of brand and state-based recognition – not only for stores but for whole areas and states – is a powerful way to keep leaders focused and motivated. This also goes a long way towards building a sense of 'community' at the area level.

Monthly recognition needs to be delivered publicly to top-performing stores and top-performing areas (acknowledging the area leaders and their areas). Recognition should be given to the highest performers and the most improved (compared with the same month of the previous year, for example). When you reward improvement you allow everyone to compete against their own previous results as well as against each other.

The public recognition also contributes to healthy competition, not only between stores but also between areas.

The value of a coffee catch-up

Lived lessons in leadership

I have facilitated my Ultimate Area Leader program, with more than 700 area leaders. On the second day of the four-day program, area leaders are given 'home-play' (a positive spin on 'homework'), for which they are to conduct ten coffee catch-ups with ten team members from their area in the month before we reconvene for day three of the program. The purpose of the coffee catch-ups is for the area leaders to get to know their people, especially their assistant managers and casual team members. This is also very good use of the area leaders' time in stores, with them having an opportunity to better understand the career ambitions of their team members and to receive feedback about what the store, area and business could be doing better.

When the group of area leaders reconvenes a month later for day three of my program, each member of the group reports back on what occurred in their coffee catch-ups. Overwhelmingly, the groups always share positive outcomes from these experiences – some of which have included the following.

- The discovery of casual team members who were unhappy in their roles and have been about to resign – but, as a result of open and constructive conversation, have had their issues resolved which led to them staying with the business
- Several assistant manager and manager roles being filled as a result of career conversations being had and team members with the desire to step up into leadership roles being discovered.

But, undoubtedly, the most positive and life-changing outcome I have heard to result from a coffee catch-up was when it was discovered that Johnny, a casual team member, was living out of his car and using the local caravan park to shower. Johnny was considered a very good performer and a highly valued team member.

Having become aware of his plight, his area leader was able to move Johnny to another store where he took on an assistant manager role. Johnny was able to get a glowing work reference which enabled him to rent an apartment.

The coffee catch-up had made a significant difference in that young man's life!

Overwhelmingly, many area leaders have achieved many positive business outcomes from having coffee catch-ups, but those catch-ups have also provided area leaders with a different perspective in regard to their own roles and have enabled them to appreciate that their team members are humans first and employees second.

The 'home-play' coffee catch-ups, as described in 'Lived lessons in leadership' above, are aimed at area leaders building a sense of community within their area and getting to know their people at a human level.

Area leaders always express amazement at how their coffee catch-ups led to career discussions, which led to casuals being promoted to fill assistant manager roles; and assistant managers being promoted to manager roles.

There have also been many stories recounted of people who were thinking of resigning but who were inspired to stay as a result of changes resulting from coffee catch-ups with their area leaders.

Aside from assisting with succession planning and the filling of roles, coffee catch-ups create an opportunity for team members to be made to feel 'invested in' and heard.

This continues to apply further up the leadership ladder. Many area leaders I have worked with had a high need for growth and left their roles to take on more senior roles with other retailers. Often, this happened because conversations mapping out a career path for them never took place, and their career aspirations and need for growth were never identified.

Every senior leader should have a clear picture of the career aspirations of their team members and should provide opportunities for those team members to develop the skills necessary to prepare them for their next role in the business.

Light bulbs

Actions

Chapter 11

The intergenerational workplace

Working with many senior retail leaders (many of whom I interviewed during my research for this book) has highlighted to me some of the challenges and frustrations they face in leading people from various generations and desperately trying to provide an environment that can help them all succeed.

I do not profess to be an expert in the intricacies of what characterises people from different generations, but I appreciate that there are intergenerational differences and I have experienced those differences when leaders from a variety of generations have taken part in my programs. I am also the parent of two Gen Z boys.

It is important to shed some light on how generational differences can affect the workplace. Research can assist leaders to reach an understanding and appreciation of the differences between the generations, so they can see the positive attributes of people from each generation rather than just being frustrated by them.

The names for the generations

The following headings provide the names usually used to describe the commonly recognised generations and the approximate spans of birth years with which they are usually associated. These do vary, depending on the source, meaning that there is no conclusive delineation of the precise years referred to by each generation name, so the spans of years in the following list can only be considered approximate (which is why the tilde [~], meaning 'approximately', has been included before them each time). The archetypal characteristics associated with each generation have also been included, but remember that these are generalisations and not *every* person from each generation conforms to these stereotypes.

THE GREATEST GENERATION: BORN ~1901–1924

These are the people who endured the hardships of two World Wars and the Great Depression, making them financially conservative/frugal. This generation displayed resilience and the ability to accept personal responsibility; they valued integrity, commitment and humility; and their work ethic laid the foundations for the future enjoyed by the generations that followed.

THE SILENT GENERATION (ALSO KNOWN AS THE TRADITIONALISTS): BORN ~1925–1945

Fewer in number than some other generations, these are the people who grew up in the shadow of the Great Depression and World War II. The global circumstances in which they grew-up led them to be hard workers who were determined and resilient in the face of adversity. It also led them to appreciate economic comfort and stability, and to be financially prudent. Respectful and courteous, they defer to those in authority and form positive relationships with both colleagues and customers.

THE BABY BOOMER GENERATION: BORN ~1946–1964

The post-war population boom of which this generation is a part fuelled an accompanying economic boom, resulting in increased housing, construction and infrastructure. People of this generation display confidence, self-assurance, independence and a social conscience which questions the way things have been in the past. They work hard and display loyalty and commitment to their employers and to the responsibilities of their own roles. They can be competitive and motivated by promotion, prestige and the potential perks of career advancement.

GENERATION X (ALSO KNOWN AS THE LATCHKEY GENERATION): BORN ~1965–1979

These were the least-parented children when compared to the generations before them. Gen X children often fended for themselves after school until their parents arrived home from work. As a result, they are independent, self-reliant, creative and resourceful, thriving on challenges and responsibility. They also value their private time away from work and are very easy-going. Born into a time of economic prosperity, large numbers of this generation are entrepreneurial and many became property owners at an early age.

MILLENNIALS (ALSO KNOWN AS GENERATION Y): BORN ~1980–1994

This is the generation impacted by the 9/11 terrorist attacks, war in Afghanistan and Iraq, the threat of 'weapons of mass destruction', the global financial crisis, and environmental issues like climate change and global warming.

Rapid increases in online communication methods have made Gen Y very tech savvy. They are adaptive, open to change, receptive to learning new things and are prepared to question their superiors if they feel it is warranted. Often they are the ones who find creative solutions to problems. They protect their work/life balance and many of them prefer flexibility in their workplace and their work schedules.

Their preference in a supervisor or manager is for a mentor with whom they can connect. They enjoy working collaboratively and are ambitious, but it is the results achieved (not the hours worked or the money earned) that are important – as are rewards and praise for the achievement of those results.

This generation has refined taste, despite the economic environment being less positive than it was in the past and the fact that many of them struggle with student debt.

GENERATION Z: BORN ~1995–2012

People from Gen Z display some characteristics similar to those of Gen Y but, along with communication skills and approachability, they also appreciate empathy as a trait in their leaders. They are hardworking, energetically creative, innovative and ambitious and prefer to work independently to achieve desired results if the goals and strategy have been communicated to them clearly. But they are also aware of the dangers of burnout and of the importance of preserving their own wellbeing, so are protective of their personal time and try to manage their work hours to achieve a satisfactory work-life balance.

They are most comfortable in a workplace which supports diversity, equity and inclusion.

Thanks to the internet and social media, Gen Z is the first truly globally-connected generation but the economic inconsistencies and societal transformations they have lived through have made them more prone to anxiety than previous generations, and more conservative. They are pragmatists rather than idealists.

While capable of splitting their focus and multi-tasking, they also have a shorter concentration span than people from previous generations. They can display resilience, despite a less than positive outlook on life, and want their lives to matter and to make a difference – so, to them, their work is about more than the money they earn. It is important to them that the organisations for which they work are ethical and socially responsible. They desire to be fulfilled and to own a home and become secure but, like Gen Y, many of them are dealing with student debt.

Being part of an inclusive supportive community is important to them and, despite being part of a digital technological generation that is heavily reliant on smartphones, they do favour face-to-face communication.

GENERATION ALPHA: BORN ~2013–2025

This is the most recent generation – and the first to have been born completely in the twenty-first century. With technological development and the redefining changes to the way we live caused by COVID 19, these people are experiencing life in a whole new way from previous generations (economically, socially, educationally and psychologically). They will grow up as globally connected, tech savvy social media influencers – but they will feel the constraints of a volatile economy and rising prices.

Rewarding and recognising people from different generations

In the workplace, as is true in the community at large and in households and families, people from different generations interact. Business leaders need to appreciate the differences evident between people from different generations and to communicate, connect, and engage with those people in different ways if their business is to succeed in the long-term.

It is also important to understand *how* to reward and recognise people from the different generations.

Leaders can only lead their teams effectively by recognising and acknowledging the different generations represented. This is about bridging gaps and appreciating as strengths the different ways that people from different generations approach things, without allowing those differences to become frustrations.

Two special cases: Gen Y and Gen Z

The retail industry has a predominantly young workforce. Millennials (Gen Y people; born between 1980and 1994) and Gen Z people (born between 1995 and 2012) will be leaders in your business over the next few years – if they aren't already! It is also very possible that you already have several Gen Z leaders in your business.

It is also likely that a Gen X leader (born between 1965 and 1979) is leading Gen Z leaders.

MILLENNIALS/GENERATION Y

On the whole, cash rewards and bonuses seem to be appreciated by the millennials/Gen Y, along with flexible hours and the convenience of the location of their workplace. They appreciate leaders who are approachable and communicate clearly.

Being dependable and ethical themselves, they also respect leaders who display integrity and who are accountable for their leadership decisions and actions.

Gen Y people are highly motivated and like to work collaboratively to achieve results as part of a team, so recognition of their team's achievements is valued more by them than recognition of their personal efforts. Opportunities to learn and develop are also highly valued.

GENERATION Z

While important, money doesn't appear to be the greatest motivator for Gen Z people – they are keen to develop and progress and appreciate opportunities to learn and develop. If opportunities for personal and professional advancement are offered, Gen Z will remain loyal to the business despite financial enticement to go elsewhere.

Leading Generation Z: The misunderstood generation

Without generalising too much and oversimplifying the situation, I do want to say that Generation Z people seem to be the source of many frustrations I hear expressed by their Gen X and Gen Y leaders.

Gen X and Gen Y leaders can struggle to lead Gen Z if they don't understand what is important to them and what they are looking to achieve from their careers. What many Gen Z individuals appear to be desperately looking for is communication, connection, and growth. From what I have seen, they are not really all that different from previous generations in terms of what they need, but it's *how* retail leaders deliver on each of their needs that must be approached differently when dealing with Gen Z.

One of my Gen X CEO clients shared with me recently that one of his Gen Z marketing managers informed him he would need to work from home for a few days because he had a new puppy and wanted to be home to help the puppy settle in! It would be fair to say that the subsequent conversation between the CEO and that manager didn't go too well. However, from my experience, this appears to be a typical example of the way different generations can have different needs and priorities.

Attracting, engaging and retaining Gen Z talent

Speaking with hundreds of retail workers, from casual Gen Z team members to the senior leaders leading them, I have found that the following suggestions assist in making the most of Gen Z talent in the workplace.

1. Ensure that you invest in and keep updated with the latest technology.
2. Create and maintain an inclusive work culture and environment.
3. Implement efficient time management.
4. Prioritise wellbeing.
5. Provide clear career development opportunities.

The suggestions from the list are discussed in more detail on the following pages and there is more about communicating with Gen Z people at the end this chapter (pages 171–5).

TECHNOLOGY

Generation Z is the first generation to grow up with easy access to digital technology from an early age. As a result of this, Gen Z workers bring unique expectations to the workplace, and have personal preferences to enhance their efficiency, improve customer service, and streamline operations.

Your businesses will benefit greatly if your Gen Z employees are given all the tools with which they are familiar and that they need to get the job done. This will include tools to make it easy to modify and communicate rosters to include consideration of their availability and preferences; and communication tools, such as messaging apps, team collaboration platforms and internal social networks which will enhance collaboration among teams.

AN INCLUSIVE WORK CULTURE

More and more retailers are understanding the need to invest in diverse hiring practices and to actively recruit candidates from a variety of backgrounds, using targeted efforts to attract people from diverse talent pools.

Flexible scheduling options are needed to accommodate the diverse needs of your workforce, such as childcare responsibilities, university commitments, religious observances, or transportation limitations (especially if you have a younger workforce).

Ensure that members of your store teams are provided with training to ensure the customer service they offer is respectful and inclusive. All customers need to be treated with respect and diverse customer needs and preferences need to be accommodated. Fellow workers need to be treated with the same kinds of consideration.

WORK LIFE BALANCE

Gen Z people value their time away from work and display the mindset that 'My work must fit into my life', which contrasts with the attitude evident in people from some of the previous generations who considered that the rest of their lives needed to be made to fit in around work. During the early days of building my career, it was seen as an indication of commitment to the job if people worked longer hours than required, regardless of whether results were being achieved or not.

Gen Z people do want to work hard, but the idea of working longer hours to get the job done is not something people from this generation understand. Helping Gen Z leaders be more efficient with their time is key, as is a change in expectations so you are prepared to reward the quality of the work done rather than the quantity of time worked.

WELLBEING

Leaders in the retail industry need to recognise and address the stressors that come with working in that industry. Recognise and appreciate all team members for their hard work and dedication, especially during busy retail seasons.

Many members of the large casual workforce employed in retail are juggling work with studies or family commitments, so they need to receive their rosters in a timely manner and to have the ability to swap inconvenient shifts easily.

Provide access to mental health resources, such as employee assistance programs and counselling services. Create a culture in which team members feel comfortable going to their leaders when they need support.

Allow and encourage store managers to organise team-building activities aimed at strengthening relationships and connection among team members.

CAREER PLANNING AND DEVELOPMENT OPPORTUNITIES

Gen Z people need to be able to see a clear career path, regardless of whether they aspire to be leaders in senior roles or not. They need to feel that they are being invested in.

Almost every retail senior leader I have worked with started as a casual and none of them had anticipated they would carve out a successful career as a retail leader. Almost all of them also shared with me that there had been one particular leader who had believed in them and helped them see a bright future ahead for them in retail.

All senior leaders should be carrying out regular career planning with their team members, from casuals to store managers, to area leaders and senior leaders. This should be undertaken by the respective leaders to whom each person reports. To assist with these regular career planning initiatives, there exist some excellent technology platforms, tools, and support systems that retail leaders can utilise.

Communication with Gen Z

As part of my research for this book, I interviewed several CEOs and general managers (who were mainly from Gen X, born about 1965–1978). One of the greatest challenges they expressed to me was understanding how to lead the workforce's newest generation. They wanted to know how to lead the Gen Z workers in their teams so that their needs were met (see pages 168–71) and they could perform at their best. I have shared my perspective on this matter with them and have attempted to help them explore the kind of workplace environment that would maximise Gen Z's performance – and I have even done my bit to debunk some commonly held myths about Gen Z.

While Gen Z people have much in common with their millennial predecessors who have been the core of the workforce for the past two and a half decades, they also stand apart from them in the many ways already discussed in this chapter. Without intending to resort to stereotyping, some of those differences mean that the approach to effective communication with Gen Z also needs to differ from communication with people from the other generations.

It would be a mistake to treat Generation Z in the same way as you would millennials and others from previous generations – because they *are* different. Developing an understanding of the Gen Z members of your team and their employment expectations and attitude to jobs is how to get the most out of them

So, how do we communicate best with this generation? As I stated earlier in this chapter, I don't claim to be an expert on this topic but I am the mother of two Gen Z boys and, in recent years, have trained Gen Z area leaders (as well as millennials), so personal experience has shown me that communication with Gen Z people needs to be handled differently.

Generation Z is the first generation to witness the birth and development of digital technology and heavily involve themselves with it. Tagged as 'digital natives', Gen Z's preferences for communication appear to be via text messages and video calls on social media platforms. If that makes you think they would also prefer online communication at work, think again! That thinking has been shown to be wrong.

While texting may be the preferred method of communication for Gen Z, one-on-one communication seems to be the most effective way of reaching them in the workplace. As leaders, it is essential that we remember to maintain personal interaction, understanding and connection in our communication.

Following are some tips that might help you.

Helpful tips

The information on the following pages discusses what have been shown to be the best ways to communicate with these young Gen Z workers.

1   DAILY FACE-TO-FACE COMMUNICATION

- Almost every member of Gen Z owns a smartphone[15] and about 50% of Gen Z people spend an average of 10 hours per day online.[16]
- Instant messaging is exalted among people from this generation but, in regard to their work environment, statistics show that 72% of

---

15 Young, K., 17 October 2017, 'Chart of the day: 98% of Gen Z own a smartphone', *GlobalWebIndex (GWI)*, 2024, viewed 7 August 2024, <https://blog.gwi.com/chart-of-the-day/98-percent-of-gen-z-own-a-smartphone>.

16 Granados, B., 22 June 2017, 'Gen Z media consumption: It's a lifestyle, not just entertainment', *Forbes*, viewed 7 August 2024, <https://www.forbes.com/sites/nelsongranados/2017/06/20/gen-z-media-consumption-its-a-lifestyle-not-just-entertainment/?sh=7d1138f18c94>.

Gen Z workers prefer face-to-face communication with their boss and team members.[17]

- In the workplace, about 40% of Gen Z people expect daily feedback from their bosses on their performance.[18] Lack of constant interaction with the higher-ups can make them feel something is wrong, negatively impacting their attitude and performance.

- Gen Z people prefer face-to-face communication at work because it is a sign that they are being taken seriously by baby boomers and millennials who hold senior roles.

2   BE HONEST AND TRANSPARENT

- Having honest, transparent conversations with members of Generation Z is vital in winning their trust and dedication. One reason they prefer in-person communication is because it is easier to detect whether someone is being straightforward with them when they are face-to-face.

- When dealing with Gen Z people, don't 'butter them up' unnecessarily and don't gloss over facts. Let them know that they can trust you to be honest with them, which will lead them to trust your leadership.

- About 80% of Gen Z people believe that being aware of their shortcomings and subsequently embracing their failures will help them improve.[19]

- More than any other generation, members of Gen Z value transparency. Do not attempt to hide wrongdoings and

17 Done, P., 24 October 2023, 'How companies can help Gen Z thrive in the workplace', *Forbes*, viewed 7 August 2024, <https://www.forbes.com/sites/forbesbusinesscouncil/2023/10/24/how-companies-can-help-gen-z-thrive-in-the-workplace/?sh=71e05bad5f84>.

18 Concordia University (St Paul), no date, 'Generation Z in the workforce', *CSP Global*, viewed 7 August 2024, <https://online.csp.edu/resources/infographic/generation-z-in-the-workforce>.

19 Ernst & Young, 18 September 2018, 'Failure drives innovation, according to EY survey on Gen Z', *PR Newswire*, viewed 7 August 2024, <https://www.prnewswire.com/news-releases/failure-drives-innovation-according-to-ey-survey-on-gen-z-300714436.html>.

mismanagement issues. Embrace open and transparent discussions at all levels by:

- having a monthly team meeting to keep everyone up-to-date and to address company-wide issues and opportunities
- opening a company social channel to boost interactions between team members
- setting up a centralised place for instant access to the brand's documents, policies, and procedures.

3   TREAT YOUR GEN Z PEOPLE AS THE EQUALS OF ALL OTHERS

- Members of Generation Z advocate equal treatment, so they don't expect the age gap between them and the previous generations to cause even the slightest disrespect or condescension. They want to be able to give their opinions and be respected.
- To treat Gen Z team members as equals at work, you should:
  - provide adequate training for them to learn new skills
  - pave a clear career path to enable development in their career
  - refrain from invalidating their complaints and/or suggestions
  - listen to them and pay attention to what they're offering to the brand.

4   MAXIMISE ONLINE COMMUNICATION CHANNELS

- No matter how much Gen Z people prefer in-person communication at work, digital communication still plays a prominent part in their lives. By blending in-person and digital communication when dealing with them, you will establish and maintain the benefits of physical interaction and also connect with them in their digital comfort zone.
- Don't resort to just using emails. Integrate workplace platforms to boost communication and collaboration.

5   USE A 'BOTTOM-UP' APPROACH

- The 'bottom-up' approach involves giving team members from all levels of the business (including Gen Z team members) a voice in providing feedback that helps with decision-making. This form of inclusivity will foster a good relationship between you and your Gen Z team members. Providing them with an active role in the business's process makes them feel free to communicate their ideas and concerns to you.

- Many retailers have implemented an open-door policy in their work environment to encourage all team members to provide feedback and to prevent the organisational hierarchy from limiting communication. Together, everyone can make the most informed decisions to improve results.

6   INVEST IN TECHNOLOGY

- Technology plays an integral part in communication in retail and one of the greatest challenges is using it to communicate in a meaningful way that gains traction.

- It is becoming increasingly challenging to send an email to a Gen Z team member and expect a quick response. However, sharing the same message on an in-house platform or via social media might be a more effective method.

I am not a technology expert, but this is the one area that retail will need to invest in continually and is something I have learned to embrace and adapt to in my own communication.

Light bulbs

Actions

Chapter 12

A system for communicating

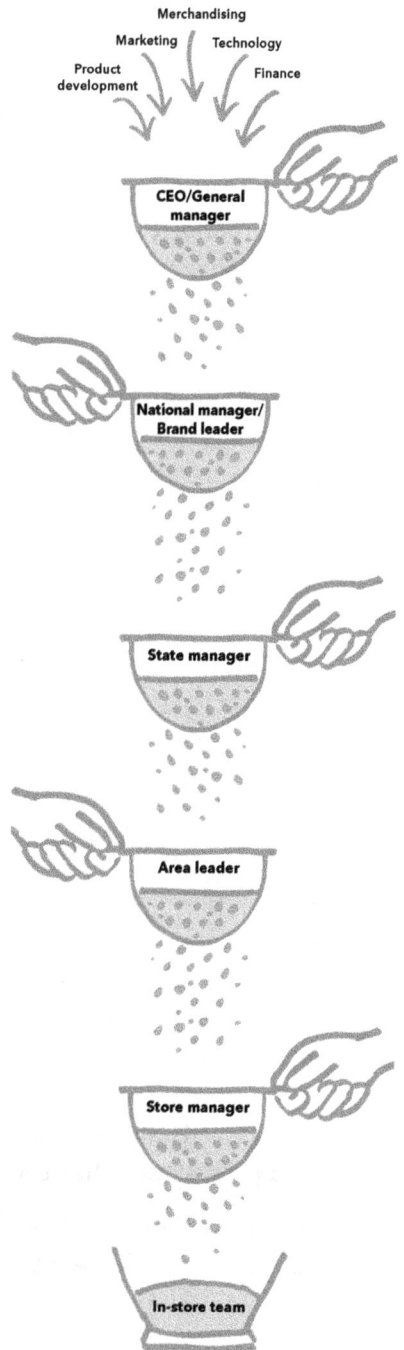

Merchandising
Marketing
Technology
Product development
Finance

CEO/General manager

National manager/ Brand leader

State manager

Area leader

Store manager

In-store team

Having worked with retailers of all shapes and sizes, I have found that several experience the same challenges regarding communication across the business. Some of these are caused by:

- people who perform different functions within the business (particularly product, development merchandising and marketing) operating in what I call 'silos' (see Chapter 5, 'Alignment with goals and plans')

- people across the business, from the senior leadership team through to the in-store teams, not being clear about the business's goals and strategies or not working in alignment with them

- using too many different channels of communication, which causes confusion and makes it difficult for people to be certain they are staying up to date

- short-term thinking, which makes any decisions that are made very reactive

- support team members being out of touch with the challenges facing stores.

The sieve model of communication

If you have ever baked a cake, you will be familiar with how most recipes instruct you to sift all the dry ingredients together through a sieve to combine them thoroughly and eliminate the unpleasant lumpy bits. Whether the recipe requires flour, castor sugar, salt, baking powder, baking soda, cocoa, or other dry powdered ingredients, all those ingredients are placed into the top of a sieve and are sifted together so they combine and fall lightly and effortlessly through the sieve.

When it comes to communication, I see the role of each level of leadership as equivalent to the part played by the sieve when preparing ingredients for baking.

From CEO/general manager, down through national leader/brand leader, state managers, area leaders and store managers, people at each level of leadership need to ensure that information is sifted to the next level in the leadership chain.

Brand leaders/national leaders are responsible for ensuring all the important information from various parts of the business and its support functions (such as marketing, merchandising, product development, human resources, technology, and finance) are sifted together and eventually reach the store managers to ensure they are all informed. With each level of leadership acting as a 'sieve' for the business, all leaders need to understand the responsibility they have to filter out the 'lumpy bits' and ensure all the *necessary* information is passed on from them to the next level in the chain. The 'lumpy bits' left behind and not filtered through to the next level will be those pieces of information that may not be necessary or appropriate for people at that next level to know (for example, highly sensitive information that does not affect them directly).

Establishing a good communication system

When it comes to communication, I often use the term 'quality over quantity'. It is not the amount of communication but its clarity and efficiency that matters. The importance of having an effective communication system needs to be understood and appreciated. Clear communication assists with engagement and means everyone feels informed and involved, which assists with aligning all of the business's people with the same purpose and goals (see Chapter 5, 'Alignment with goals and plans').

Leaders need to develop communication skills for different types of conversations if they are to achieve successful business outcomes.

Lived lessons in leadership

When leading 'VicMania' (see pages 12–13 and 60), I would hold quarterly, two-day, off-site planning retreats for the area leaders and leaders of the support teams. I held the first of these retreats when I was very new to that 'Vicmania' leadership role.

As well as being aimed at working on our strategy for the quarter ahead, my quarterly retreats were designed to build a positive workplace environment by focusing on relationships and connection. The time spent at the retreats, and the information shared, ensured every area leader knew precisely what our financial goals were for the quarter ahead and what each area was responsible for achieving to contribute to that overall goal. We would work on strategies together, which helped provide consistency and clarity, as well as suitable support for both new and experienced area leaders alike.

Area leaders who were achieving well in regard to specific KPIs would be invited to share with the group what they were doing to achieve their results. This opportunity to share their methods of success not only contributed to making those area leaders feel significant in the business but also provided invaluable advice from which the other area leaders could learn.

I would very rarely book hotels or conference centres for the retreats because those venues were too costly. I would select a location no more than ninety minutes away from Melbourne and would book a house or cabins big enough to accommodate all of us. We would all pitch in and do our own catering. Area leaders would be paired up to shop for the ingredients, and to prepare and cook each meal for the whole group. This not only made the retreat cost-effective but also contributed to connection and team building.

At the end of every two-day planning retreat, all the area leaders and state-based support leaders walked away with their own clear ninety-day plan and everyone was aligned with the same overall strategy and business plan. This made it easier for me to follow up progress with each individual area leader during our one-on-ones and planning sessions throughout the quarter.

Having the area leaders together for two days each quarter saved a great deal of time that otherwise would have been spent dealing with issues due to a lack of clarity or expectation.

Despite the other advantages gained, I would say the biggest impact of the retreats was the human connection and sense of belonging that was created. Some of the most memorable times I had at Flight Centre were during quarterly planning retreats.

Holding a similar planning retreat was almost the last thing I did eight years later when I finished in the role of 'Vicmania' leader.

State manager and area leader monthly planning sessions

At the end of each month, state managers should have a planning session with their area leader team. This is the time to review the month's results, recognise great achievements, brainstorm solutions for any significant challenges and ensure everyone is prepared for the month ahead.

Monthly planning sessions will often focus on operations but should also follow the direction of and progress towards the goals and plans everyone committed to at the quarterly planning retreat (see pages 80–81). Reflect on the month that has been and plan for the month ahead, ensuring the strategies are on track to achieve the quarterly goals. The aim of every planning session is for area leaders to leave feeling inspired and focused for the month ahead.

These sessions are not about 'updates'. Apart from helping ensure everyone is on the same page and aligned to the same goals, the aim should be to focus on challenges, address what needs adjusting and find solutions, especially if the month's results are less than expected.

One-on-ones

MONTHLY ONE-ON-ONES

Monthly one-on-ones between individual leaders and their direct reports at all levels of the business enable them to work on specific strategies, ensuring that expectations are met and appropriate support and feedback are provided. These one-on-one discussions allow everyone to be accountable for their results. Ideally, the one-on-ones should take place near a store so that you both can visit the store. You may be strategic about where you choose to meet. For example, it may be near an underperforming store which will enable you to provide feedback to that store when you visit together. Or it could be close to a store that is achieving outstanding results that you want to acknowledge and recognise.

State managers and area leader monthly one-on-ones

I want to highlight particularly that each state manager (or whoever area leaders report to) should meet with their individual area leaders once a month to follow up on progress and address any issues in regard to the commitments made during the monthly planning sessions. Meetings with area leaders new to the role and those whose results indicate they might need support should be the priority, but all area leaders do need to have the benefit of this one-on-one discussion time every month because everything I have shared about agreed business strategies and achieving goals will rely heavily on area leaders for implementation.

PERFORMANCE CONVERSATIONS

Performance conversations can be challenging at times, regardless of seniority. This is because you are a human being who has emotions and you are dealing with other human beings who also have emotions. Fear of how these conversations could be heard and interpreted can often hold leaders back from having them, despite them being necessary.

Leaders for whom the need to be liked is paramount are more likely to be uncomfortable involving themselves in effective performance conversations. In the extreme, depending on what is said, there can also be a fear of the law and litigation, so leaders with concerns of that kind don't have conversations about performance at all and just hope that performance will gradually improve.

You may also be familiar with the term 'soft skills' sometimes used to refer to people skills, which include good communication and interpersonal skills. Yet, for many leaders, the term 'soft skills' is a misnomer. There is nothing that can be considered 'soft' about delivering a performance conversation. Any conversation in which an assessment of someone's performance is delivered will be complicated and the reactions to it can often be unpredictable, simply because it involves people, their emotions and their reactions.

You may also have heard or used the term 'difficult conversations'. I prefer to avoid this term because it presupposes that conversations about performance will be difficult. I prefer the term 'honest conversation'. To help your team members improve, you need to provide them with honest feedback.

If you ensure people are clear about what you expect of them, then it is easier to have performance conversations.

FEEDBACK CONVERSATIONS

According to Sue Anderson, author of *Feedback Fitness: Three simple steps for leaders to have courageous conversations that drive performance,*[20] feedback drives performance. So feedback conversations and performance conversations are closely related.

Leaders are in a great position to create a culture wherein feedback occurs in a series of ongoing conversations, not as a series of separate awkward speeches. Sue Anderson has said:

> *As well as cultivating a culture of connection, trust and psychological safety so feedback conversations can occur organically . . . leaders can set up the systems to ensure feedback conversations are embedded into the existing meetings. By adding feedback conversations to the agendas of all existing meetings, such as team meetings or regular one-on-one[s] . . . leaders are sending the clear message that feedback is valued, welcomed and expected.*[21]

IMPACTFUL ONE-ON-ONES

To help ensure your one-on-ones have the desired impact, they:

- need to be well-planned and well-prepared
- can be used as a follow up to the monthly planning sessions (see page 182), to ensure each area leader is aligned to the business's goals for the month ahead
- should prioritise which area leaders need to be seen first, based on their level of experience and their current results
- should be used as a development opportunity
- should be held at a location close to a store, so that a store visit can also be done. (But remember that the purpose is to spend time with the area leader, not the store teams in the stores.)
- can be carried out online when face-to-face is not possible.

---

20 Anderson, S., *Feedback Fitness: Three simple steps for leaders to have courageous conversations that drive performance*, Good2gr8 Coaching, Melbourne, 2024.

21 Anderson, S., Personal email communication with Alison Crabb, 19 March 2024.

Weekly trade meetings

Gathering key people for weekly meetings and updates typically happens on a Monday. Many senior retail leaders will admit that, though these meetings happen every week, it is with varying levels of effectiveness. To make Monday trade meetings more effective, they require structure and preparation. If the structure for communication I recommend is implemented effectively, weekly trade meetings may not be necessary – however, the people involved in each business will need to decide if this is the case.

These meetings should start by reflecting on the week that has passed, but there needs to be a more consistent and structured approach employed for the rest of the meeting. Meetings should finish with recognition of weekly milestones and ensure that everyone will be continuing to do everything for which they have committed to be accountable.

Here are some tips to help trade meetings have more impact.

- Ensure you are clear on why you are having the meetings in the first place; which means ensuring you have clear outcomes in mind for every meeting.
- Spend time planning, to ensure the meetings will follow a logical structure.
- When discussing results, focus on which specific actions and strategies did or did not achieve those results.
- Avoid meetings going off track and ceasing to be focused on and aligned with agreed goals and plans.
- Ensure the discussion ends with a clear plan of action.
- Ensure you are holding everyone accountable for delivering on strategies.

CREATING A CONSISTENT STRUCTURE

Each week, ask everyone attending the meeting to reflect and bring along answers to the following questions:

- What did I achieve this week?
- What worked well this week?
- What didn't work well this week?
- What milestones did I achieve this week?
- If we could rewind and do this week again, what would I do differently?
- What have I learned that I will take into next week?
- What are the team's goals for the week to come?
- How do we support each other and remove any hurdles/roadblocks limiting success?
- Are there any other decisions we need to make as a team?

Why store manager meetings are crucial to results

If there were one strategy I would implore every retailer (regardless of size, location, or current results) to adopt for improving results, it would be for area leaders to have monthly face-to-face meetings with store managers. Those meetings would be the quickest and most impactful way to circulate information to store managers and to improve communication.

I want to emphasise that I am referring to area-based meetings, for which the store managers from each area come together. These are *not* state-based meetings extending to include people from beyond each area leader's area of influence.

Store manager meetings might be time-consuming for area leaders to plan and execute, but they are the greatest source of engagement, problem-solving and strategic planning for the month ahead. Though they are often seen as costly, these meetings are the greatest cost-saving tool available to retailers and are certain to impact results positively. The meetings need to be considered 'business meetings', elevating the significance of the store managers' role. They also provide an opportunity for store managers to build a sense of community and connection with other store managers. For all these reasons, I consider these meetings among the most powerful and productive investments of money, time and effort a retailer can make.

Although this book is aimed at assisting senior retail leaders, it is also designed to remove hurdles and roadblocks faced by many other leaders when implementing change and attempting improvements to the way they execute their roles.

At the beginning of this chapter, I shared a sieve analogy as a model of communication in business. Store manager meetings play a crucial role in ensuring that information flows smoothly from one level of the business to the next, in the way illustrated by that sieve example.

Earlier in this book (see pages 54–61) I shared the benefits of implementing strategies to meet the 'six core human needs' and the critical role those needs can play in devising your strategy for engaging, retaining, and developing your people, especially store managers.

Holding store manager meetings is one single strategy that can be implemented to fulfil every one of the 'six human needs'. The table on the next page summarises how.

STORE MANAGER MEETINGS AND THE 'SIX HUMAN NEEDS'	
THE NEED	**HOW THE NEED IS MET**
Certainty	• Meetings are held in the first few days of *every* month for no longer than three hours. • Timely business updates on results and strategy are provided. • Each monthly meeting should follow a similar structure. • Opportunities are provided for store managers to ask questions to gain clarity.
Variety	• Store managers have time away from being constrained between the four walls of their stores. • Different venues, located near stores in the region, are used to hold the meetings. • Development is provided on different aspects of the store manager role.
Significance	• Great performances for the month are acknowledged. • Store managers achieving great results are asked to present to the group. • Each store manager's role is 'elevated' by attending monthly 'business meetings'.
Connection	• Relationships between store managers are forged and improved. • Store managers provide more support to each other in their day-to-day operations. • Store managers feel part of a larger community, rather than just leading their own stores in isolation.
Contribution	• Store managers can share strategies that are working and are also able to collaborate and develop new ones. • Store managers can support each other and become less reliant on their area leader. • Store managers work towards the area's monthly goals and strategies.
Growth	• The meeting offers opportunities for learning, development, and training. • Store managers can learn from each other. • Store managers can be observed and those individuals having potential for more senior roles can be identified.

I can hear you wondering what the cost to your business would be to implement monthly store manager meetings. I believe that the costs of not holding these meetings can be even greater.

Following is an exercise for you to complete to help you assess the cost versus the benefit of monthly, face-to-face, store manager meetings.

Using the template below, itemise the costs of everything required for area leaders to hold a typical face-to-face monthly meeting with store managers. Think of every possible cost associated with the meeting, so you can arrive at an accurate idea of its overall cost. Even if you believe it would be unrealistic for store managers from regional locations to attend each month, for the purpose of this exercise, please assume they would be attending.

Some of the costs I have listed below may not be necessary, but for the purpose of the exercise, I have listed as many possibilities as I could.

COST OF A STORE MANAGER MEETING	
ITEM	**COST**
Transport for attendees	$
Accommodation for anyone needing to travel a long distance	$
Venue hire	$
Breakfast; or snacks, coffees, etc.	$
Wages for people to cover store managers' shifts while they are out of the store	$
Any other associated costs (list them below):	
	$
	$
	$

Once you have calculated the total cost for one monthly meeting, multiply it by twelve (months) to arrive at an idea of the total annual cost for one area holding a monthly face-to-face store manager meeting.

If you lead multiple area leaders you could do this exercise for each of their areas to arrive at an understanding of total costs versus benefits for each area. Adding together the figures for all of your areas will give you the annual cost of these meetings for the whole business.

ANNUAL COST OF STORE MANAGER MEETINGS FOR ONE AREA

Cost per meeting per month $ _____ × 12 months = _____ (annual cost)

Full-year **area** revenue: $_____

What percentage of the annual revenue equates
to the cost of twelve store manager meetings: _____%

Cost versus benefits of holding monthly store manager meetings:

_____

_____

_____

_____

_____

_____

_____

I have done this costing activity many times with area leaders and the leaders of area leaders. Once they have been able to put 'cost versus benefit' in context, they realise how small the cost of store manager meetings are in comparison to the benefits they provide and they see that those meetings are well worth the investment. Usually, the cost of holding a monthly face-to-face meeting is less than 0.005% of sales revenue.

The remaining barrier to acceptance by area leaders is convincing their own leaders that the benefits of these meetings outweigh the cost, thereby gaining their approval for the meetings to be scheduled.

As you read this, I hope I have also convinced you of the benefits of this strategy so you will consider implementing it.

Allowing these meetings to be scheduled is often a big decision for business leaders. If you are open to this but still concerned about the cost, I recommend piloting store manager meetings for three months in two areas – your most successful area and your most underperforming area. This will allow you to gauge the impact the meetings can have in regard to two distinctly different scenarios. You can then make an informed decision as to whether this is a strategy you would like to implement long-term.

Preparing and delivering successful store manager meetings

The Ultimate Area Leader program I facilitate covers, in detail, how area leaders can plan, prepare and facilitate great store manager meetings. But there are a few tips I can provide here to help you support area leaders and ensure they maximise the opportunities the meetings provide.

- Store manager meetings should be held as early as possible at the beginning of each month. This allows everyone to focus quickly on the new month. (Regular scheduling contributes to meeting the core need for 'certainty', see page 55.) The meeting should be held face-to-face but, if it isn't possible to have all store managers at the meeting, some meetings will need to be held online. Hold the online meeting as a separate meeting and not at the same time as your face-to-face meeting.

- You may be more comfortable holding monthly store manager meetings online to reduce costs; however, it is important to note that online meetings do not meet all of the six core human needs in the same way face-to-face meetings do.

- Build a culture in which the people in stores can appreciate that they contribute to the overall area results (meeting the core need of 'contribution', see page 55), rather than each store team seeing their own budget and results in isolation.
- Acknowledge the results achieved by the whole area as well as individual store results (meeting the core need of 'contribution', see page 55).
- Acknowledge and reward great individual and store performances (meeting the core need of 'significance', see page 55) – setting an example to which all the other store managers can aspire.
- Store meetings should be two to three hours long – no longer. They must be short, sharp and on-point to set up for the month ahead.
- The meetings should be organised and well prepared, so allow the area leaders adequate time to prepare for them. Some suggestions for what needs to be prepared before the meeting include:
  - advice for store managers about any information they need to prepare to bring to the meeting regarding a specific strategy or outcome on which you want to focus (circulated to the store managers in a timely fashion so they have adequate time to prepare before the meeting)
  - a review of the previous month's minutes and agenda – so the area leaders know what they were expected to follow up from that meeting
  - details of the results for the total area as well as individual stores
  - details of the wins and positive outcomes for the area
- Encourage area leaders to predetermine some outcomes they would like each store manager to take from the meeting. Encourage them to ask themselves:
  - What specifically do I want to achieve from this meeting?
  - What do I want my store managers to have committed to when they walk away from the meeting?

- Encourage area leaders to keep their focus consistent. There is no need for new focuses and strategies every month. For example, if retention is a key focus, that may be presented as a strategy every month.

- Encourage area leaders to invite guest presenters or experts from within the business to their store manager meetings, to help with aspects of the business on which the store managers need to focus (for example, marketing, product development, or merchandising).

- Store managers who are achieving great results, should be invited to present to the others what they believe is assisting in delivering those results (again meeting the core need of 'significance', see page 55). Store managers enjoy hearing from other store managers and this is a great way to support their development.

- Store manager meetings are intended to be positive and focused on solutions. They are not the place to air issues and grievances (that is best done in one-on-ones).

- Store manager meetings provide a great opportunity for workshopping and sharing ideas to improve the store managers' business acumen and leadership skills (meeting the core need for 'growth', see page 55).

- Strategies from store manager meetings should be followed up during one-on-ones and store visits. Area leaders can tell from the one-on-one discussions whether store managers are engaged and displaying a greater level of ownership.

For store managers to take more ownership and be accountable and responsible for their results, you must elevate how you see their role and treat them like 'spiritual business owners'. There is no doubt that having monthly store manager meetings achieves this.

Summarising the approach for state leaders and area leaders

The following table outlines the communication methods I recommend specifically between state leaders and area leaders. You can adjust these suggestions to suit your business's size and structure.

ALIGNING GOALS AND PLANS: STATE LEADERS AND AREA LEADERS			
LED BY	**TYPE OF COMMUNICATION**	**WHO ATTENDS**	**WHEN**
Brand leader/State manager	**Trade meeting** • Each support function and operations leader provides an update and ensures everything is on track to achieve the goals for the month. • Address any potential hurdles or roadblocks to achieving results. • Make the meeting meaningful and powerful. Don't just 'tick the box' indicating that a trade meeting has been held.	Brand leader, state manager relevant support function leaders and area leaders	Weekly
Area leader	**Store manager meetings** • Utilise collaborative problem-solving opportunities. • Review the results of the past month and plan for the month ahead. • Review the month's area results. • Recognise great area results. • Disseminate information to store managers. • Build community and connection between store managers.	Area leader and store managers	Monthly

Light bulbs

Actions

Chapter 13

You, your time and resources

In preparation for this book, I interviewed several senior leaders from various retailers, including CEOs, general managers, brand leaders, state managers and area leaders. Many openly shared some of the frustrations they experience and how overwhelmed they sometimes feel. The demands on senior leaders in retail can be relentless – particularly when results are not in line with expectations.

This book is intended to support senior retail leaders in navigating the complexities of retail leadership. I hope, as you have read through these pages, you have been able to reflect on what is working well in your business and what opportunities you can identify that will assist you to lead differently.

I also hope you have been provided with food for thought regarding new approaches, new ways of thinking, new areas of focus, and new strategies to implement.

How you manage yourself does play a significant part in how you manage others – and the way you *lead* yourself will have a considerable impact on the way you lead others.

Lived lessons in leadership

At the height of my retail career, I was leading 212 stores and 1400 people across four retail brands. I had eleven area leaders reporting to me and forty-five support team members performing various functions within a support team leadership structure.

Most weeks I felt like I was on a treadmill that I would step onto on Monday mornings and then step down from on a Friday afternoon. I would then spend every weekend recuperating, ready to do it all again the following week.

At the time, I also had two boys in high school. Fortunately, my very supportive husband Shane took care of most things at home.

I started to see that the relentless way I was working was unsustainable, I was putting the needs of everyone with whom I worked ahead of my own needs and that was forcing me to work longer hours. I felt guilty when I was at work because I thought I should be at home, and when I was home I felt guilty because I felt that I should be at work.

This was also a time when my best friend Rachel was diagnosed with lymphoma. Her ways of working were very similar to my own and her illness gave me the wake-up call I needed. Observing and acknowledging the changes she was forced to make helped me to transform the way I was working.

The age-old metaphor, derived from air travel, of putting my own oxygen mask on first before assisting others, was exactly what I needed to do.

Many of the changes I made at that time have already been expounded and recommended throughout this book, especially in the area of communication and empowering leaders to make more decisions and back themselves.

I began to focus more on myself, including prioritising my health and wellbeing. I began regular strength-based exercise, ate a healthy diet that included more plant-based foods, and drank less alcohol and more water. I would attend a health retreat annually and committed to educating myself on what it took to lead a healthier life. I also made significant changes to my morning routine so I could get every day off to a great start.

I started to lead my team by example, especially ensuring the area leaders were maintaining a better work/life balance and that everything we did together focused on 'quality over quantity'.

My health and wellbeing still remain my highest priority and the decisions and changes I made back then have become my way of life. They also have proven to have been the best decisions I could have made for both my family and my business.

Build a frictionless life at home

The more demanding your work role becomes, the busier you will be and the less you will focus on yourself. Is now the time to get your life in order and prioritise how you lead yourself?

When I realised that I needed to care more about how I led myself, I first looked at what I could 'outsource' at home. I worked out what my hourly pay rate equated to and looked at what my husband and I did at home that we could outsource to someone who would cost less per hour than we were earning. Some of the changes resulting from this included engaging a fortnightly cleaner and outsourcing our ironing to someone who would pick up and drop off the clothes every week. I set up direct debits for all bills, so they were automatically paid, rather than us having to spend time on weekends paying them. Simple changes such as these made a massive difference to our weekends. When I was home, I was able to be more present with my family.

In the workplace, it comes down to how well you manage your time and use your resources (particularly the people you lead) to help you get the job done.

Wellbeing and performance expert Alessandra Edwards has emphasised to me that self-care is crucial for personal health and effective leadership:

In the demanding realm of retail, leaders face unique pressures that can impact their performance and their team members. . . Biologically, the stress of leadership roles can lead to increased levels of cortisol which, over time, can impair cognitive function, reduce resilience, and lead to burnout. By prioritising their wellbeing, leaders can regulate their stress responses, maintaining clarity and decision-making prowess even under pressure.

Moreover, leaders who model a commitment to self-care inspire their teams to adopt similar practices, fostering a healthier, more productive work environment. A balanced lifestyle, incorporating physical activity and mental health practices, supports neural growth and emotional regulation, essential for navigating the complexities of the retail industry with agility and insight. . . [I]ntegrating self-care into one's leadership approach is not merely about personal health; it's a strategic element of professional excellence, enhancing both individual performance and organisational outcomes. This holistic approach ensures leaders not only survive the rigours of their roles but thrive, setting a benchmark for success.

By adopting this perspective, leaders can create a positive ripple effect, promoting a culture where wellbeing is intertwined with peak performance, ultimately driving sustainable success for themselves and their teams.[22]

Take the time to reflect on your own approach to leadership, based on what you have read in this book. Assess what is working for you and the people you lead, and what is not. Decide how your role, actions and decisions are

22 Edwards, A., Personal email communication with Alison Crabb, 14 March 2024.

impacting your wellbeing. Determine any improvements you could make – for the benefit of both yourself, your family and the team.

In the table below, enter what reflecting on your leadership approach has helped you identify as your current approaches and behaviours. Also include new approaches for potential improvement. Tick the boxes to indicate whether you want to 'Keep' or 'Stop' each existing trait or action, or 'Start' something new.

INFLUENCES ON MY LEADERSHIP AND WELLBEING			
ACTIONS, BEHAVIOURS AND APPROACHES	KEEP	STOP	START

Light bulbs

Actions

Part 4:

Conclusion

My aim for this book is to inspire you with innovative and thought-provoking strategies designed to ignite meaningful discussions within your leadership team.

It is hoped that implementing the strategies using the insights you have gained will enhance your personal growth, elevate the impact of your leadership, and assist you in achieving better results and forming better connections with the people you lead.

On the following two pages, take the opportunity to write down the strategies and suggestions that have resonated with you most. Reflect on how these insights have shifted your perspective on leadership, then outline the specific actions you plan to take to implement those strategies within your business. Use that space to map out your journey towards setting a higher standard of leadership for yourself and the members of your team.

Light bulbs

Actions

Afterword: Work with me

As was the case for my first book, *The essential guide for area leaders in retail*, my hope for this book is that reading it might be the catalyst you need to make changes in the way you lead. If change for the better is what you seek, then implementing some of what you have read here will assist.

I am committed to working with retail leaders to deliver genuine growth in the people they lead and to deliver outstanding results for their businesses.

If you would like to develop your leadership skills further, I extend an invitation to you to work with me. You can do this in various ways. All the information in this book can be unpacked and developed further through workshops, programs, keynote presentations and one-on-one coaching sessions.

If you are part of a larger retailer network and would like to discuss a bespoke program for your retail leadership team, please get in touch.

Visit my website: www.alisoncrabb.com.au

Contact me: alison@alisoncrabb.com.au

MENTOR AND COACHING PROGRAMS

A feature of great leaders is that they never stop learning. Mentorship and coaching for leaders are a sound business investment.

While the specific challenges faced by individual leaders vary, the one-on-one coaching process invariably allows leaders to improve their capabilities and results, experience greater satisfaction, and become at ease in their roles by making them more skilled and ready to respond to opportunities as they arise.

You can benefit from complete access to my experience, expertise and support from the training programs I offer, or from bespoke coaching programs I design to focus on your individual needs over a timeframe that suits your goals.

WORKSHOPS

If any element of your business appears to be limiting the engagement or performance of the people you lead, my workshops are designed to get your business moving quickly towards better results.

I personally facilitate every session, ensuring that the learning is tailored to your needs and you have not only the benefit of my expertise but also my direct support.

Over time, I have observed the incredible impact targeted training can have on the areas which hold businesses back. Half-day and full-day workshops can be tailored to target issues faced by your business, to ensure that the best outcomes for you are achieved.

LEADERSHIP PROGRAMS

My leadership programs have been designed to elevate retail leadership to a new level. As much as we all want to achieve results, those results are really the outcome of how well we manage to provide a happy and productive workplace environment and implement our business strategies.

My leadership programs expand and elaborate on the contents of this book, providing deeper understanding and learning, in a timeframe that allows you to work on one strategic consideration at a time.

KEYNOTE SPEAKING AND CONFERENCE WORKSHOPS

Do you have an upcoming conference you would like to use as a vehicle to provide training for your team?

My delivery of keynote presentations and group training at conferences has proven to be an effective way for me to share inspirational, actionable insights with diverse audiences.

As a tailored offering, my presentations can be adapted to reflect your organisation's conference theme and key focuses.

For more details visit: www.alisoncrabb.com.au

Testimonials

. . . the team were hugely grateful for the time you spent with us; you continue to absolutely resonate with who we are and how we operate. Everybody got something worthwhile. . . we are better because of the time you spent with us.

Brett Blundy
(BBRC, Chairman and founder)

I want to thank Alison for her incredible teachings and for inspiring me personally and professionally.

I now have a work-life balance I've never had in the ten years I have been leading. I have never felt more connected within a region; importantly, I've never seen a team more connected with each other.

Ashleigh Lindsay
(Spendless Shoes Pty Ltd, Retail leader,
ACT, NSW, Victoria and Tasmania)

Alison's program did not disappoint. It is rare that you have the opportunity to partner with someone who has performed a role, led people in the same role and now develops people in [that] role.

. . . [T]he area leadership program has allowed us to create a shared way of working that elevates the impact of leadership in our business . . .

Sally Craig
(Kennards Hire,
General manager: People and Culture)

Alison's sessions have [resulted in] powerful and immediate day-to-day changes and have given . . . myself and my team a better understanding of the role and [the] best practices for . . . [performing it]. I [now] understand the skillset and behavioural attributes to succeed in the role and better support those transitioning from store manager to area manager. Alison's motivation to see leaders thrive in their field is obvious, genuine and inspiring. My team and I will take some truly powerful learnings with us forever.

Laura Barrett
(The Athlete's Foot, State manager)

Alison helped me better understand what drives my people, which has helped me create a positive culture with increased engagement and motivation across my team. I can help my team feel more in control of their workload and set up for success.

Amanda Evans

(Hype DC Pty Ltd, State manager)

Alison supports the business on multiple levels. As HR manager, I value having an objective perspective on some of the challenges we've faced ... Alison has worked with us extensively on senior leader performance, and each area leader was noticeably more positive and focused after each of their one-on-ones. We have an open and honest working relationship that I truly value.

Alison is an empathetic, inspirational leader who has assisted us in working towards a team-first culture ...

Kyla Smith

(The Pancake Parlour, HR manager)

Working with Alison taught me key fundamentals of being a great leader.

I have gained a high level of confidence in my leadership, allowing me not to second guess myself as much as I used to.

I always leave any coaching session with a clear idea of my next objectives and the knowledge that I will be held accountable for them.

Samuel Fragapane

(All Green Nursery & Garden, General manager)

There is no one I know that is more qualified, experienced and successful when it comes to working with retail teams than Alison. Her book is a must-read for anyone who is leading retail teams ...

Donna McGeorge

(author, trainer, facilitator)

Glossary

'accommodating' area leaders	a category of area leaders who provide their store managers and team members with high levels of support but have low expectations for the store/area results, being more concerned with relationships than results
area leader	a business employee whose role it is to oversee several retail outlets within an organisation (sometimes called a multi-site manager; a regional leader; a regional manager or a cluster manager)
assistant store manager	the store employee employed in a supporting position to a store manager and having the potential to become a store manager in the future
brand	a name, term, design, symbol, or any other feature that identifies one retailer's goods or services as distinct from those of other retailers
brand leader	a leader responsible at a national level for all aspects of a particular brand, usually in a multi-brand retail business
brand manager	*see* brand leader
business strategy	*see* strategy
CEO	chief executive officer; the person ultimately responsible for making major decisions, and driving the direction and strategy to achieve business success
cluster manager	a person whose role is similar to that of an area leader but who is responsible for a smaller group of stores and is, occasionally, still leading a store

'controlling' area leaders	a category of area leaders who provide their store managers and team members with low levels of support but have high expectations for store/area results, tending to take over control at store level to achieve desired results
conversion rates	measures of the proportion of visitors to a retail outlet who make a purchase
'empowering' area leaders	a category of area leaders who provide their store managers and teams with high levels of support and have high expectations for the store/area results, striking a happy balance between a harmonious work environment and strategies to achieve results
engagement	the connection and motivation that team members have for performing their best at work each day
environment	as well as referring to the surrounding circumstances, objects, or conditions in the usual way, the term is used in this book to refer to the intangible, unquantifiable quality of a workplace and work situation that makes somewhere a good place to work
exit interview	a final interview with a departing team member
fixed mindset	the belief that there is no opportunity for change or improvement
general manager	a person reporting directly to the CEO in larger businesses, who is responsible for delivering the strategy to achieve business success
growth mindset	the belief that continual growth and development occur with openness to change and possibilities; and that we have the capacity to improve and grow
key performance indicators (KPIs)	quantifiable measures used to evaluate the success of a business or individual in meeting objectives

level up — to progress or advance to the next level

margin — the differences between the price a retailer pays for an item and the price at which the item is sold to customers

merchandising — the activity of promoting the sale of goods, especially by their presentation in retail outlets

multi-site manager — *see area leader*

national leader — *see brand leader*

national manager — *see brand leader*

one-on-ones — a regular check-in between two people within an organisation – typically a manager and a team member

regional leader — *see area leader*

regional manager — *see area leader*

retention — the ability to ensure team members stay with the business and don't feel the need to leave or to find employment elsewhere

'stagnating' area leaders — a category of area leaders who provide their store managers and team members with low levels of support and have low expectations for store/ area results

state leader — *see state manager*

state manager — the leader who oversees and leads the area leaders and whose region includes all the smaller areas/ regions in a state. These leaders are responsible for a range of activities, including education, professional development, policy, advocacy, communication, marketing, sponsorship, finance and administration

store manager	the person in a managerial role in a store who is responsible for team members and their wellbeing; presentation of marketing and store displays; recruitment, performance management and customer experience
strategy	a summary of how the organisation will achieve its goals, meet the expectations of its customers, and sustain a competitive advantage in the marketplace
support (provided by senior leaders)	delivery to leadership teams, who are from lower levels on the seniority ladder, of the tools and training they require to do their jobs and deliver on expectations
support teams	the individuals (from areas such as finance, payroll, product development, marketing, merchandising, operations and human resources) whose duties generally include performing administrative tasks, understanding and adhering to the policies and procedures of the business, making recommendations for improving the customer experience, developing strategies to increase the company results, and encouraging a positive work ethic
SWOT days	days for support teams to spend time in stores focusing on determining **s**trengths, **w**eaknesses, **o**pportunities and **t**hreats, as well as ways in which issues could be resolved
team leader	*see* store manager
turnover	the rate at which team members leave the business
working *on* business (WOB) days	contrasting with 'working *in* business' days, these are days spent planning and reflecting (rather than working in the field)

About the author

Alison Crabb is recognised by many as the industry's leading expert on retail leadership. In her role as the principal of Alison Crabb Consulting, Alison has designed a unique, refreshing, personalised and highly engaging, retail-centric approach to leadership training and development. Her thirty years of experience in consumer-led retail have provided her with invaluable insights into the factors influencing retail success and the keys to achieving and delivering it.

Alison's career in the retail industry began as a travel consultant with the Flight Centre Travel Group, where her promotion – first to store manager and then to an area leadership role – eventually saw her spend eight years as a global leader in a highly competitive and challenging retail environment.

Through those years of learning, development and improvement, Alison continued to push the boundaries and drive improvement year on year, seeing profit grow from $18 million to $49 million. The culture of excellence Alison was instrumental in building at Flight Centre during her years of leadership led to her division being the most profitable division globally for eight consecutive years. She achieved unprecedented results working with more than 1200 people across more than 200 retail outlets, generating $1.2 billion in sales annually.

In 2010, Alison's achievements were recognised with Flight Centre's Directors' Award for Global Outstanding Achievement. She was also a finalist in the Telstra Businesswoman of the Year Award in 2012 and has been a judge of the 'Outstanding Growth' category of the Telstra Best of Business Awards since 2022.

Alison works with some of Australia's leading retail businesses, providing coaching, training, and development – including facilitating leadership workshops, programs, and keynote addresses, focused on developing and lifting their leadership teams to achieve new business heights. Throughout her career, Alison's business reputation has been built on sound foundations of knowledge, experience, trust, and success.

For more details, visit: www.alisoncrabb.com.au

or email Alison: alison@alisoncrabb.com.au

By the same author

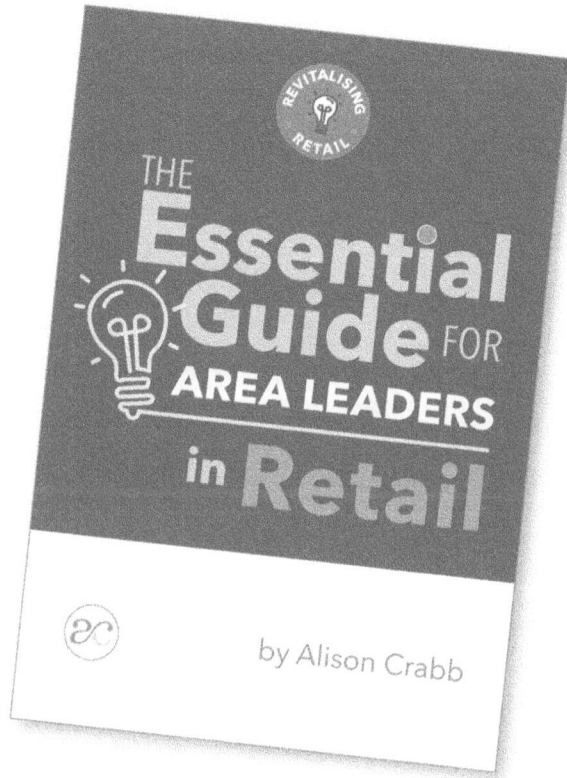

by Alison Crabb

AVAILABLE FROM:

https://alisoncrabb.com.au/product/the-essential-guide-for-area-leaders-in-retail

www.ingramcontent.com/pod-product-compliance
Lightning Source LLC
Chambersburg PA
CBHW080247030426
42334CB00023BA/2730